Quilts Galore!
QUILTMAKING STYLES
AND TECHNIQUES

Quilts Galore!

QUILTMAKING STYLES AND TECHNIQUES

Diana McClun and Laura Nownes

THE QUILT DIGEST PRESS

Project direction by Michael Kile.
Editorial direction by Harold Nadel.
Book and cover design by Kajun Graphics.
Quilt photographs by Karen Steffens and Sharon Risedorph.
Room setting photographs by Sharon Risedorph.
Cover photograph by John Clayton.
Computer graphics by Kandy Petersen. Hand-drawn graphics by Marilyn Hill.
Hand-drawn templates by Adele Ingraham.
Typographical composition by Rock & Jones and DC Typography.
Printed by Nissha Printing Company, Ltd., Kyoto, Japan. Color separations by the printer.

Hand appliqué and trapunto instructions overseen by Adele Ingraham.
Machine appliqué instructions overseen by Katie Prindle.
Stenciling instructions overseen by Ren Brown.
Crazy quilt instructions overseen by Claire Jarratt.
Quiltmaking techniques and ideas shared by Lucille Hilty, Mary Ellen Hopkins,
Kay Huston, Arlene Lane and Kandy Petersen.
Quilting and sewing assistance by Sandy Klop, Katie Prindle and Anna Venti.
Invaluable review of drafting exercises by Sally Barlow, Lisa McClun,
Mary Helen Schwyn and Lari Smith.
Patterns graciously lent by Jinny Beyer, Kay Huston, Adele Ingraham,
Arlene Lane, Mary K. Ryan, Shirley A. Shenk and Jan Snelling.
Pattern name consultation by Barbara Brackman.
Technical assistance by Thomas V. Smith.

Room stylings by Michael Kile and Jeff Bartee.
Assisted by Diana McClun, Tricia Thomas and Bernice Stone.
Homes graciously lent by Mardell Pinckney, Pauline Elizabeth Stone and Tricia and Steven P. Thomas.

*Diana wishes to thank her husband David for his enthusiasm and encouragement;
Laura, for warmth, joy and meticulous labors; the many quilters who shared their expertise and creativity;
and Michael and Harold, for their vision, confidence and wisdom.*

*Laura wishes to thank her husband Bill and good friends Harold and Kandy for all their
hard work and support which helped to make this book a reality.*

Third printing.

Library of Congress Cataloging-in-Publication Data

McClun, Diana, 1934-
    Quilts galore! : quiltmaking styles and techniques / Diana McClun
and Laura Nownes.
        p.   cm.
    Includes index.
    ISBN 0-913327-21-2 : $19.95
    1. Quilting—Patterns.   2. Machine quilting—Patterns.
I. Nownes, Laura, 1953-   . II. Title.
TT835.M399   1990
746.9'7—dc20   90-42209
                                                CIP

The Quilt Digest Press
P.O. Box 1331
Gualala, CA 95445

On the bed, see page 100. On the wall, see page 115. On the chest (foreground), see page 72. ▶

HOME OF PAULINE ELIZABETH STONE

See page 155.

See page 114.

See page 103.

See page 161.

See page 52.

On the wall, see page 80. On the couch (foreground), see page 142

See page 132.

See page 62.

See page 50.

TABLE OF CONTENTS

CHAPTER 1

DRAFTING

 How many times have you looked through a book or magazine, seen a quilt that appealed to you so much that you immediately wanted to make it, but found your enthusiasm disappear when you could find no pattern or instructions? If this experience sounds familiar and you want to do something about it, this chapter on drafting pieced quilt block patterns is for you.

Drafting is a skill often overlooked by quilters; many feel intimidated, and uneasy about attempting it. They do not see it as a necessary tool or recognize its many advantages. But learning to draft will allow you better to understand the more intimate details of balance, shape and design in pieced quilt blocks. Any pieced quilt pattern can be drafted (an outline made of the shapes of the block) onto a piece of graph paper. With a little time, effort and practice, and the use of the proper tools, drafting is an easy process. Once a pattern has been drafted, you can make individual pattern parts (called templates) from template plastic and use them to make your quilt.

The advantages of drafting are numerous:
• You can make pieced patterns in any desired size.
• You will no longer be limited to the pattern size found in this or any other book.
• You can make your own pattern when one is not available.
• It encourages creativity, giving you the opportunity and knowledge necessary to design your own original quilt patterns.
• It will give you a more precise idea of how a block is constructed, so you can see the relationship between its parts and the whole.

This chapter will acquaint you with the grid system used to categorize pieced block patterns and will provide you with eight practice exercises for drafting pieced block patterns. A class outline is given at the end of the chapter; and it is intended to be used as a guide for self-teaching or by instructors in a classroom setting.

By working with the grid system described below, you can accurately draw squares, rectangles, triangles and diamonds onto a piece of graph paper. These shapes are the basic parts for most pieced quilt block patterns. We will discuss the three main types of pieced block patterns: symmetrical, asymmetrical and circular. These will be further broken down according to their basic parts and their placement onto the grid system.

THE GRID SYSTEM

For our purposes, a grid is a larger square broken down into smaller squares of uniform size. Most traditional pieced quilt block patterns can be placed into categories based upon the grid system. With an understanding of the grid system you will be better able to see and draft the individual shapes contained in most quilt block patterns.

GRID CATEGORIES

One Patch: Those patterns which repeat a singular shape (such as a square, rectangle, triangle or hexagon) over and over.

Four Patch: Those patterns which divide into four equal squares.

Other blocks falling into this category can be broken down even further by dividing each of the squares into quarters to form 16 equal squares.

These 16 divisions can be further broken down to form a block containing 64 equal squares.

Five Patch: Those patterns which divide into 25 equal squares.

Seven Patch: Those patterns which divide into 49 equal squares.

Eight-Pointed Star: Those patterns which radiate from the center.

Nine Patch: Those patterns which divide into nine equal squares.

Other blocks falling into this category can be broken down even further by dividing each of the squares into quarters to form 36 equal squares.

Circular: Those patterns which are derived from a circle.

Other blocks not falling into the grid system include houses, flowers, animals, etc.

MARKING A GRID

Drafting begins with marking an accurate square, the finished size of your block, onto a piece of graph paper. This is a simple task, as the graph paper provides a grid of squares of uniform size and accurate 90-degree angles. You can use a pencil and large C-Thru ruler to follow the guide lines on the paper. In most cases, once you have marked the outer edges of your block, you can simply follow the lines on the graph paper to fill in the individual template shapes. With a little practice, you will soon be able to examine a pieced block pattern, identify the grid category and draft the individual template shapes.

In most cases it will not be necessary to mark the outline of the grid. There are some instances, however, when the grid markings will not line up exactly with the graph paper. In these cases it will be helpful to mark the grid lines *before* filling in the individual shapes. Marking a grid is a relatively simple task. You would have no trouble marking a grid for a Five Patch pattern within a 10″ block. Each square of the grid will measure 2″ on each side.

Determining the size of each square within the grid is easy when the block is easily divisible by the grid size: for example, 10″ (block size) divided by 5 (number of squares across the grid) = 2″ (size of each square within the grid).

There may be an instance when you want to make a Five Patch pattern in a 9″ block (or any other block size which is not easily divisible by 5). The following method will allow you to mark an accurate grid within any size block. This is a very useful and easy technique, which Laura's sister learned in a graphics design course and passed on to her.

Using the example of a Five Patch grid within a 9″ block:

1. Using a lead pencil and C-Thru ruler, mark a 9″ square onto a piece of graph paper.

2. Lay your large C-Thru ruler directly below the bottom edge of the square, with the left-hand edge in line with the bottom left-hand corner of the square, exactly as shown in the diagram.

3. Holding the upper left-hand corner of the ruler in place, carefully swing the right side of the ruler up until the 10″ marking intersects the right-hand edge of the square, exactly as shown in the diagram. Make sure the upper corner of the ruler is *exactly* at the corner.

NOTE: 10″ is used because it is the next whole number greater than 9″ (block size) which is evenly divisible by 5 (number of squares across the grid).

✷ *Helpful hint:* If, when you swing the ruler, the next whole number extends beyond the right-hand edge of the square, you can extend the right-hand side of the square and place the ruler, exactly as shown in the diagram.

4. Using your pencil, mark points along the ruler every 2″, exactly as shown in the diagram.

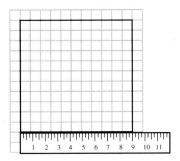

Step 2

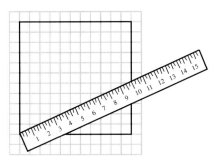

Step 3

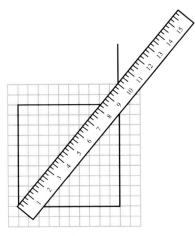

Helpful Hint

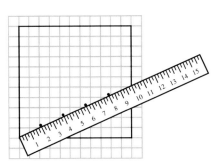

Step 4

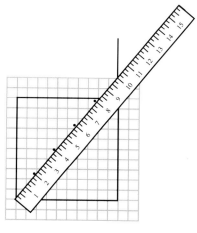

Helpful Hint

NOTE: 2″ is used because 10″ (next whole number determined in Step 3) divided by 5 (number of squares across the grid) = 2″.

✳ *Helpful hint:* If you are working with an extended right-hand edge, lay the ruler and mark points, exactly as shown in the diagram.

5. Keeping your ruler perpendicular to the top and bottom edges of the square, mark vertical lines going through the four points, exactly as shown in the diagram.

6. Turn your graph paper a one-quarter turn and repeat Steps 2 through 5. This will complete the grid, exactly as shown in the diagram.

7. You can now fill in the grid with whatever Five Patch pattern you desire, such as *Delectable Mountains*. Once the individual template shapes have been marked you can erase any unnecessary grid lines.

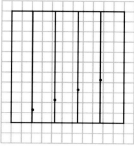

Step 5

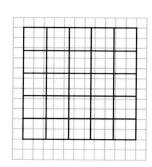

Step 6

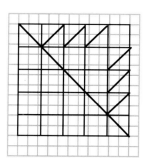

Step 7

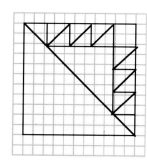

Step 7

PRACTICE EXERCISES IN DRAFTING

The practice exercises below are presented in a logical step-by-step, easy-to-follow format. After successfully completing these exercises, you will feel confident enough to practice these skills with a variety of block patterns. Using these skills will make you a more creative, flexible and knowledgeable quilter.

Knowing how to enlarge and reduce the size of pieced block patterns opens up a wide range of design possibilities. You will be able to adjust any pattern size to fit your particular design needs (or bed or wall size). You must keep in mind, however, that some patterns (because of their proportion and number of divisions) become too cluttered and difficult to construct when made too small. When size is reduced, the individual elements can become lost. On the other hand, a simple pattern made too large can become boring and the shapes, colors and lines lose their balanced inner relationship to each other. There is often a fine line between what size works well and what does not. For this reason, we suggest that you try each of the practice exercises in various sizes.

The block sizes for the following practice exercises can be drawn in any size, although in some cases suggestions are made to avoid working with awkward measurements. Experiment, avoid self-imposed limitations: use a variety of sizes.

SUPPLIES:
Graph paper, ⅛" grid
Sharp lead pencil
C-Thru plastic 2″ × 18″ ruler (B-85)
Eraser
Red ultra-fine permanent pen
Compass (for *Dutch Rose*)
Paper scissors

There are eight practice exercises: easy, intermediate and advanced for both symmetrical and asymmetrical block patterns and two lessons in drafting a circular pattern. ✳ *Helpful hint:* Work through them in the order in which they are presented. Quilts for each of the eight patterns in these exercises are found in Chapters Two and Four.

PRACTICE EXERCISES FOR SYMMETRICAL PATTERNS

✳ *Helpful hints:* To spare yourself much grief and possible frustration during your drafting experience, before you begin check the accuracy of your C-Thru ruler with the graph paper. Lay the ruler on top of the paper to see that all of the markings correspond. It is not uncommon to find an inaccurate ruler or piece of graph paper.

EASY: Drafting an *Economy* block (Grid category: Four Patch)
1. Using your C-Thru ruler and lead pencil, mark a square of any size on the graph paper. Since this is your first exercise, we suggest using an even number for ease in measuring.
2. Mark the corners A, C, E and G and center points B, D, F and H of each side of the square, exactly as shown in the diagram.
3. Mark the following lines:

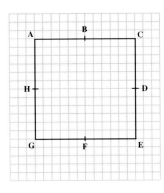

Step 2

B to D	F to H
D to F	H to B

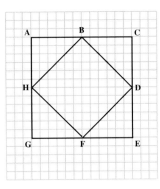

Step 3

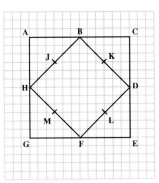

Step 4

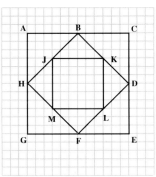

Step 5

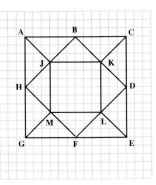

Step 6

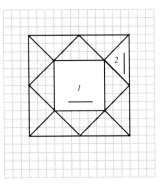

Economy with Templates

4. Find and mark the center points J, K, L and M of lines HB, BD, DF and FH, respectively, exactly as shown in the diagram.
5. Mark the following lines:

J to K	M to L
K to L	J to M

6. Mark the following lines:

A to J	E to L
C to K	G to M

This completes the *Economy* block. Notice that there are two template shapes: #1 a square and #2 a triangle. Note that all of the triangles are the same size.

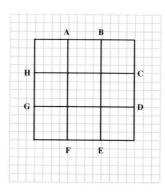

Steps 2-3

INTERMEDIATE: Drafting a *Kandy's Path* block (Grid category: Nine Patch)

1. Using your C-Thru ruler and lead pencil, mark a square of any size on your graph paper. Choose a measurement which is easily divisible by 3 to avoid working with awkward fractions; for example, choose 6″, 7½″, 9″, 10½″, 12″, or 13½″.

2. Divide the block size by 3 and use this measurement to divide the block into nine equal squares. Mark points A, B, C, D, E, F, G and H, exactly as shown in the diagram.

3. Mark the following lines:
   A to F   H to C
   B to E   G to D

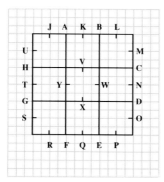

Steps 4-5

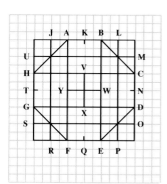

Step 6

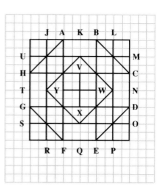

Steps 7-8

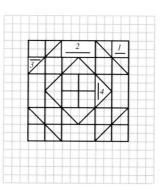

Kandy's Path with Templates

4. Mark points J, K, L, M, N, O, P, Q, R, S, T and U, which are the center points on the sides of each small square, exactly as shown in the diagram.

5. Mark points V, W, X and Y, which are the center points of lines HC, BE, GD and AF respectively, exactly as shown in the diagram.

6. Mark the following lines:
   J to R   L to P   U to M   S to O   A to H
   B to C   D to E   G to F   V to X   Y to W

7. Lay the ruler from point K to point Q (through points V and X). Place dots on lines UM and SO where the ruler crosses. Then lay the ruler from point T to point N (through points Y and W). Place dots on lines JR and LP where the ruler crosses.

8. Connect the dots marked in Step 7, exactly as shown in the diagram.

This completes the *Kandy's Path* block. Notice that there are four template shapes: #1 a square, #2 a rectangle, #3 a small triangle and #4 a large triangle.

ADVANCED: Drafting a *Dutch Rose* block (Grid category: Eight-Pointed Star)

1. Using your C-Thru ruler and pencil, mark a square of any size on your graph paper. It is best to choose a whole number 8″ or larger to avoid working with too small pieces and awkward fractions.

2. To determine the center point of the square, lightly mark diagonal lines from corner to corner, exactly as shown in the diagram.

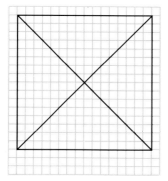

Step 2

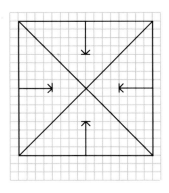

Step 3

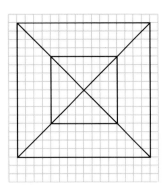

Step 4

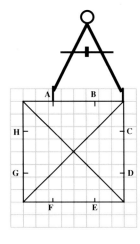

Steps 6-7

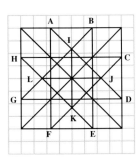

Steps 8-10

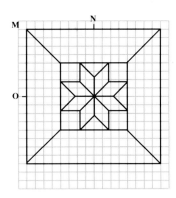

Step 11

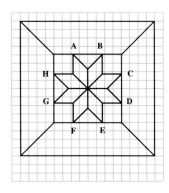

Step 12

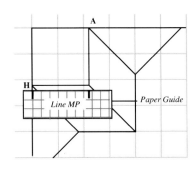

Step 13
Helpful Hint

3. Divide your block size by 4. Then use this measurement to mark a distance from each side of the square in toward the center, exactly as shown in the diagram.

4. Extend the markings made in Step 3 to form an inner square, exactly as shown in the diagram.

5. Use the compass to determine the distance from the center point of the inner square to the upper right-hand corner of the inner square.

6. Using the distance determined with the compass, mark a distance from the upper right-hand corner of the inner square to points A and D.

7. Using the same distance, continue in the same manner with the remaining three corners of the inner square to mark points B, C, E, F, G and H, exactly as shown in the diagram.

8. Mark the following lines:

| A to D | B to G | C to F | E to H |
| A to F | B to E | C to H | D to G |

9. Mark in points I, J, K and L.

10. Mark lines from I to K and J to L.

11. This completes the center star of the block. Use the eraser to eliminate the lines running through the corner squares and the diamonds.

At this point you have drafted all of the shapes required to construct the *Dutch Rose* block. Notice that the center star is the *Le Moyne Star.* If you want to make templates for an 8″ *Dutch Rose,* simply draft a 4″ *Le Moyne Star;* a 5″ *Le Moyne Star* will give the shapes required for a 10″ *Dutch Rose,* a 6″ for a 12″, etc.

12. Mark the upper left-hand corner of the outer square point M and center points N and O, exactly as shown in the diagram.

13. Use the measurement of the upper left-hand corner square of the center star to mark a distance from point M to point P, from point P to point Q, from point M to point R and from point R to point S. ✱ *Helpful hint:* Frequently, the measurement of this line does not line up exactly with the lines on your graph paper. In order to transfer the exact measurement, it is helpful to make a paper guide. Cut a strip of graph paper approximately 1″ × 3″. Place the strip directly below the bottom line of

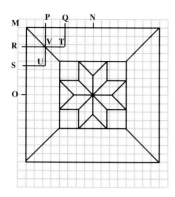

Steps 13-14

the square in the upper left-hand corner of the center star. Mark the length of this line onto the strip of graph paper, exactly as shown in the diagram. Label this paper guide line MP as it will be used for following steps. This paper guide can now be used to mark the squares required in the upper left-hand corner of the outer square. This method is more accurate than approximating the length when working with awkward measurements.

14. Use the ruler to extend lines from points Q and R to meet at point T and from points P and S to meet at point U. Mark point V, exactly as shown in the diagram.

15. Mark a line from point T to point A and from point U to point H.

16. Keeping your ruler parallel to the lines on the graph paper, mark lines the distance of your paper guide, from point N to point W and from point O to point X, exactly as shown in the diagram.

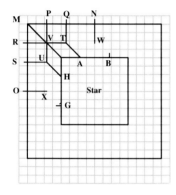

Steps 15-16

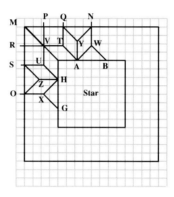

Steps 17-19

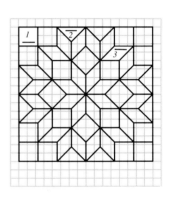

Dutch Rose with Templates

17. Mark a line from point W to point A and from point X to point H.

18. Use the paper guide to mark a distance from point A to point Y and from point H to point Z.

19. Mark the following lines:

| Q to Y | S to Z | W to B |
| N to Y | O to Z | X to G |

20. Use the eraser to eliminate lines MV, AB and HG.

21. Repeat Steps 12–19 for the remaining three corners of the block.

This completes the *Dutch Rose* block. There are three template shapes: #1 a square, #2 a triangle and #3 a diamond.

PRACTICE EXERCISES FOR ASYMMETRICAL PATTERNS

EASY: Drafting a *Delectable Mountains* block (Grid category: Five Patch)

1. Using your C-Thru ruler and lead pencil, mark a square of any size on your graph paper. Choose a size which is easily divisible by 5 to avoid working with awkward measurements; for example, choose 5″, 6¼″, 7½″, 8¾″ or 10″.

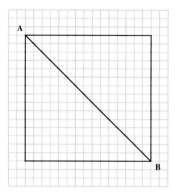

Step 2

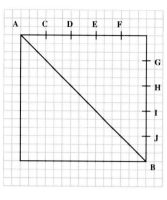

Step 3

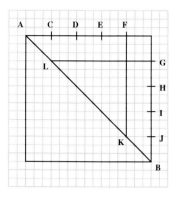

Step 4

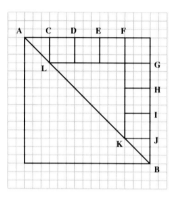

Step 5

2. Mark corners A and B and then mark a diagonal line from A to B, exactly as shown in the diagram.

3. Divide the block size by 5 and use this measurement to mark off five equal spaces this size across the top and right-hand sides of the block and mark these points C, D, E, F, G, H, I and J, exactly as shown in the diagram.

4. Mark a line from point F straight down to line AB and mark this point K, and from point G straight across to line AB and mark this point L, exactly as shown in the diagram.

5. Mark straight lines from points C, D and E to line LG and from points H, I, and J to line FK, exactly as shown in the diagram.

6. Mark diagonal lines in each of the small squares, exactly as shown in the diagram.

This completes the *Delectable Mountains* block. There are three template shapes: #1 a small triangle, #2 a medium triangle and #3 a large triangle.

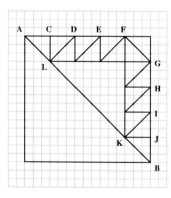

Step 6

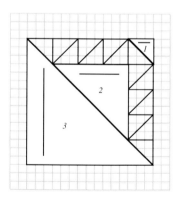

Delectable Mountains with Templates

INTERMEDIATE: Drafting an *Indian Bonnets* (*Pine Tree* variation) block (Grid category: Four Patch)

This pattern differs from other block patterns because it is not a square.

1. Using your C-Thru ruler and lead pencil, mark a square of any size on the graph paper. Choose a size that is easily divisible by 8 to avoid working with awkward measurements, for example 8″, 10″, 12″, 14″ or 16″.

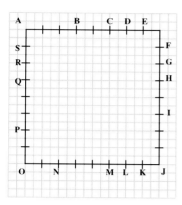

Step 2

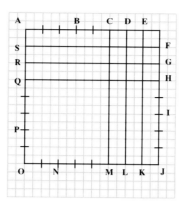

Step 3

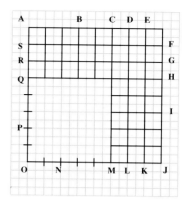

Step 4

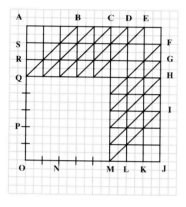

Step 5

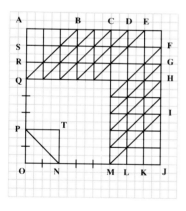

Step 6

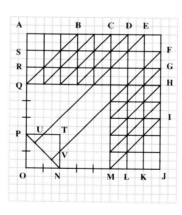

Step 7

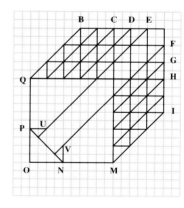

Step 8

2. Divide the block size by 8 and use this measurement to mark off eight equal spaces this size across each side of the block. For example, if your block size is 12″, mark off points every 1½″. Then label points A through S, exactly as shown in the diagram. ✷ *Helpful hint:* Note that not all points are given a letter. Double check the placement of your letters with the diagram.

3. Mark the following lines:

| C to M | D to L | E to K |
| S to F | R to G | Q to H |

4. Fill in the grid, connecting the remaining points on the top outer line to line QH and the remaining points on the right outer line to line CM, exactly as shown in the diagram.

5. Mark the appropriate diagonal lines through the grid, exactly as shown in the diagram.

6. Extend lines from point P and point N to meet at point T, forming square PTNO. Then mark a line from point P to point N, exactly as shown in the diagram.

7. Extend the diagonal lines which start at point E and point F only as far as line PN. Then mark point U at the intersection of line PT and point V at the intersection of line TN, exactly as shown in the diagram.

8. Use your eraser to eliminate lines UT, TV and triangles ABQ and IJM, exactly as shown in the diagram.

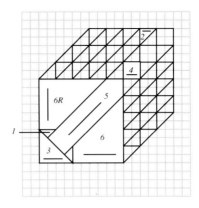

Indian Bonnets with Templates

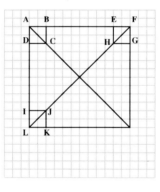

Steps 1-3

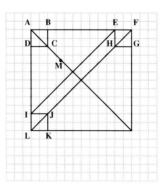

Steps 4-5

This completes the *Indian Bonnets* block. There are six template shapes: #1 a small triangle, #2 a medium triangle, #3 a large triangle, #4 a square, #5 the tree trunk and #6 the background.

ADVANCED: Drafting a *North Carolina Lily* block (Grid category: Eight-Pointed Star)

This block cannot be drafted using the traditional Eight-Pointed Star method as in *Dutch Rose*. Below is a chart which will help you in deciding on the finished size of the block you would like to draft. These particular sizes have been suggested because of their ease in keeping within the 8-to-the-inch grid system. If you desire a size other than those suggested, you will have to start by drafting the left-hand corner square and work outward to the finished block size. In many cases it will be necessary for you to work in sixteenths, which is a little more difficult but can be accomplished with accurate graph paper and C-Thru ruler. Check the C-Thru ruler against the graph paper to see that all the measurement marks line up exactly. ☐ *Warning*: Extreme accuracy is important for the success of this block. Double check to see that the ruler and paper correspond. Take time to verify your measurements at the checkpoints throughout the exercise.

Finished Block Size	Corner Square Size
7¼″	1¼″
10¼″	1¾″
12⅜″	2⅛″
15⅜″	2⅝″

1. Select a Finished Block Size you would like to draft. Then, using your C-Thru ruler and lead pencil, mark a square on the graph paper.

2. Using your C-Thru ruler and pencil, lightly mark diagonal lines through the square, exactly as shown in the diagram. These lines are used as a guide and will be erased when the block is complete.

3. Select the Corner Square Size which corresponds to your Finished Block Size and mark a square of this size in the upper left-hand corner, upper right-hand corner and lower left-hand corner of your block. Then mark points A through L, exactly as shown in the diagram.

4. Mark a line from point I to point E, exactly as shown in the diagram.

5. Lay your C-Thru ruler through points A and C for help in achieving the correct angle, then mark point M exactly as shown in the diagram. The measurement of line CM is the same as line AB. ✱ *Helpful hint*: Place a whole number marked on your ruler at point C for ease in measuring the new line. Sometimes this line will not line up exactly with the lines on your graph paper. In order to transfer the exact measurement, it is helpful to make a paper guide. Cut a strip of graph paper approximately 1″×3″. Place the strip directly below line AB. Then mark the length of this line onto the strip of graph paper, exactly as shown in the

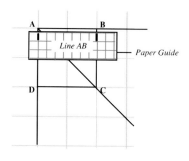

diagram. Label this paper guide line AB, as it will be used in following steps. This paper guide can now be used to mark the exact length of line CM.

6. Keeping your ruler parallel to the lines on the graph paper, use the measurement of your paper guide (line AB) to mark a distance from point M to point N and from point M to point O, exactly as shown in the diagram.

7. Mark a line from point B to point N and from point D to point O, exactly as shown in the diagram.

8. Keeping your ruler parallel to the lines on the graph paper, use your C-Thru ruler (or make a paper guide) to determine the distance from line BC to line MN, indicated by the arrow in the diagram. Then, double this measurement to mark a distance from point B to point P and from point D to point Q, exactly as shown in the diagram. ✳ *Helpful hint:* To verify that all previous steps were done carefully, lay your ruler from point Q to O to N to P; a straight line should be formed.

9. Mark a line from point N to point P and from point O to point Q, exactly as shown in the diagram.

10. Extend perpendicular lines from point P and point Q to meet at point R on line IE, exactly as shown in the diagram.

11. Use your paper guide (line AB) to mark a distance from point P to point S and from point Q to point T, exactly as shown in the diagram.

12. Mark a line from point T to point M to point S, exactly as shown in the diagram.

13. Lay your C-Thru ruler along line QR and also extend it beyond the right-hand edge of the block. Mark point U where the ruler meets the line, exactly as shown in the diagram. Using the same method, lay your ruler along line PR and mark point V where the ruler meets the bottom line of the block, exactly as shown in the diagram.

14. Mark a line from point V to point U, exactly as shown in the diagram.

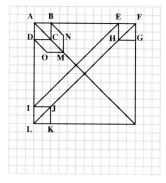

Steps 6-7

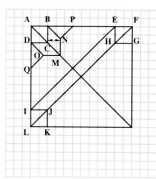

Steps 8-9

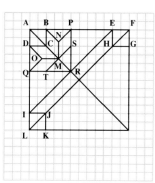

Steps 10-12

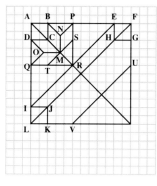

Steps 13-14

15. Lay your C-Thru ruler along line NM and extending beyond line IE. Mark point W where the ruler meets line IE. Then using the same method, lay your C-Thru ruler along line OM and mark point X where the ruler meets line IE, exactly as shown in the diagram.

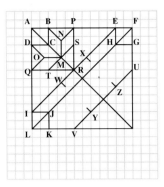

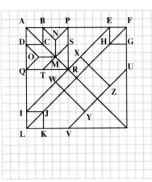

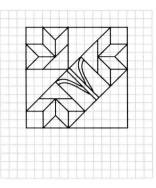

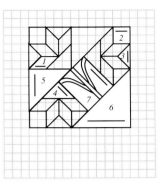

| *Steps 15-16* | *Step 17* | *Steps 18-19*
 Completed Block | *North Carolina Lily with Templates* |

16. Lay your C-Thru ruler along line IJ and extending beyond line VU. Mark point Y where the ruler meets line VU. Then using the same method, lay your C-Thru ruler along line EH and mark point Z where the ruler meets line VU, exactly as shown in the diagram.

17. Mark a line from point W to point Y and from point X to point Z, exactly as shown in the diagram.

18. At this point you have drafted all the shapes required to construct the *North Carolina Lily* block. If you would like to complete the pattern you can use the same measurements as given above for obtaining the diamonds and triangles. Notice that the flowers in the upper right-hand corner and lower left-hand corner of the block are turned on their sides. Refer to the completed diagram for the exact placement of the individual shapes.

19. Erase the lightly marked diagonal lines which were created in Step 2 above, with the exception of line CM.

20. When the block is constructed, bias strips of fabric will be sewn into rectangle WXYZ for the stems.

This completes the *North Carolina Lily* block. There are seven template shapes: #1 a diamond, #2 a square, #3 a small triangle, #4 a medium triangle, #5 a medium-large triangle, #6 a large triangle and #7 a rectangle.

Please note that the *North Carolina Lily* pattern in Chapter Two is a variation of this block. The width of the side rectangles is the measurement you used for the corner squares in drafting the block.

PRACTICE EXERCISES FOR CIRCULAR PATTERNS

EASY: Drafting a *Fan* block

1. Using your C-Thru ruler and lead pencil, mark a square of any size on your graph paper and mark points A, B, C and D, exactly as shown in the diagram. It is recommended that your block size be 6″ or larger to avoid working with too small pieces.

2. Position the tip of your compass at point C and extend the pencil end and mark a quarter-circle of any size within the square, exactly as

SUPPLIES:
Graph paper, 1/8″ grid
Sharp lead pencil
C-Thru plastic 2″ × 18″ ruler (B-85)
Red ultra-fine permanent pen
Compass
Protractor
Push pins
Cardboard, non-corrugated
Template plastic
Eraser

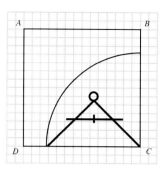

Steps 1-2

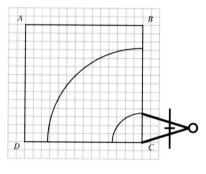

Step 3

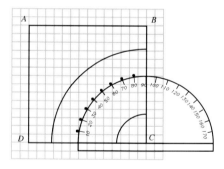

Steps 4-5

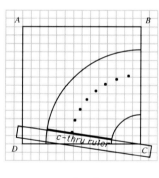

Step 6

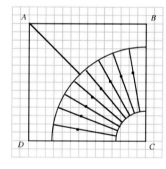

Steps 7-8

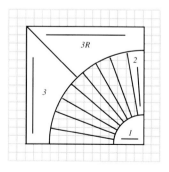

Fan with Templates

shown in the diagram. ✳ *Helpful hint:* For a good proportion, make this curve about three-fourths or more of your block size but not so large that the background shape will be difficult to piece at the two corners.

3. Keeping the tip of your compass at point C, retract the pencil end and mark a smaller quarter-circle of any size within the square, exactly as shown in the diagram. ✳ *Helpful hint:* For a good proportion, make this curve about one-fourth or less of your block size but not so small that the shape will be difficult to piece, as there will be many seams coming together in that area.

4. Lay your protractor over the square, exactly as shown in the diagram. Line CD should be in line with the 0-degree marking and line BC should be in line with the 90-degree marking.

5. The fan is divided into nine equal segments. This is easy to accomplish, because in looking at the markings on the protractor you will notice that there are nine 10-degree units within your marked square. Use your pencil to mark at each 10-degree increment (eight points), exactly as shown in the diagram.

6. Position your C-Thru ruler to intersect with both the 10-degree mark and point C. Then, draw a straight line connecting the large arc and the small arc, exactly as shown in the diagram.

7. Repeat Step 6 for the remaining segment markings, exactly as shown in the diagram.

8. Lay your C-Thru ruler to intersect points A and C, then mark a line connecting point A with the large arc, exactly as shown in the diagram.

This completes the *Fan* block. Notice that there are three template shapes: #1 the small quarter-circle, #2 the fan segment and #3 the background piece. Note that one of the background pieces must be reversed when cutting the fabric shape. Indicate this on the template shape.

ADVANCED: Drafting a *Double Wedding Ring* block

If you are like most quilters you do not have the proper drafting tools required to make large circles. The small compasses we are all familiar with do not have enough expansion to make a large ring. You can easily make your own tool with a strip of template plastic and push pins.

Presented here is only one of the many variations of the *Double Wedding Ring*. It forms a circle, whereas some are more oblong. After you become familiar with the technique, you may wish to vary the width of the pieced arcs and/or the number of segments within them.

1. Determine the size ring you would like to make, for example, 18″.

2. Divide your ring size by 2, for example, 9″.

3. Using your large C-Thru ruler and lead pencil, mark a square of this size on the graph paper.

4. Mark the corners A, B, C and D, exactly as shown in the diagram.

5. Divide your square size by 5 and use this measurement to mark a distance from point B to point E, from point B to point F, from point D to point G and from point D to point H, exactly as shown in the diagram.

✷ *Helpful hint:* If your block size is not evenly divisible by 5, round off to the nearest eighth. Use the chart below for help.

.125 = 1/8
.25 = 1/4   for example, 9 ÷ 5 = 1.8. .8 is closest to .75,
.375 = 3/8   so use 1.75 or 1¾.
.5   = 1/2
.625 = 5/8
.75 = 3/4
.875 = 7/8

6. Cut a strip of template plastic 1″ wide by at least 1″ larger than one side of your square.

7. Place a push pin through the center of one of the short ends approximately 1/4″ from the edge, exactly as shown in the diagram.

8. Lay your graph paper over the piece of cardboard. Then secure the push pin and plastic template strip at point A. Make sure that the plastic template strip lies flat against the graph paper.

9. Adjust the plastic template strip so that it lies over point E. Then use the permanent marking pen to indicate this point with a dot on the plastic template strip. This point will be used for constructing the inner arc.

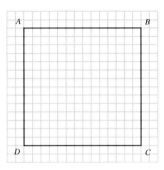

Step 4

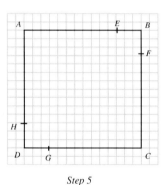

Step 5

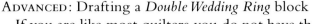

Insert push pin here

Plastic Template Strip

Step 7

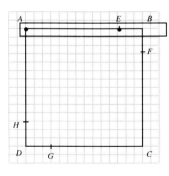

Step 9

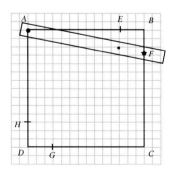

Step 10

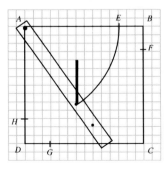

Step 12

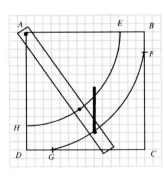

Step 13

10. Without removing the push pin, rotate the plastic template strip toward yourself until it lies over point F. Then use the permanent pen to indicate this point with a dot on the plastic template strip. This point will be used for constructing the outer arc.

11. Use the other push pin to pierce through the plastic at the two dots. Push the pin as far as it will go, as the holes must be large enough to accommodate the tip of the pencil. Remove pin.

12. With the plastic strip and push pin still secure at point A, place the tip of your pencil into the hole made for the inner arc. Starting at point E, rotate the pencil and plastic template strip around to point H, forming an arc, exactly as shown in the diagram. ✷ *Helpful hint:* Point H is simply a checkpoint. It is the end point of the arc.

13. Next, place the tip of your pencil into the hole on the plastic template strip for making the outer arc. Starting at point F, rotate the pencil and plastic strip around to point G, forming an arc, exactly as shown in the diagram. ✷ *Helpful hint:* Point G is simply a checkpoint. It is the end point of the arc.

14. Remove the push pin from point A, and secure it with the plastic template strip at point C.

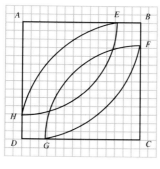

Step 15

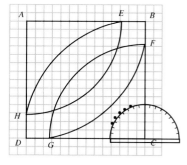

Steps 16-17

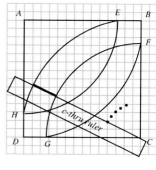

Step 18

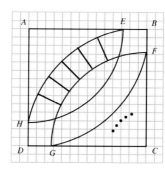

Step 19

15. Repeat Steps 12 and 13 to make an inner arc from point F to point G and an outer arc from point E to point H, exactly as shown in the diagram.

16. Lay your protractor over the square, exactly as shown in the diagram. Line DC should be in line with the 0-degree marking and line BC should be in line with the 90-degree marking.

17. Use your pencil to mark points at 25 degrees, 35 degrees, 45 degrees, 55 degrees and 65 degrees, exactly as shown in the diagram.

18. Position your C-Thru ruler to intersect with the 25-degree mark and point C and beyond the farthest arc. Then, draw a straight line between the two farthest arcs, exactly as shown in the diagram.

19. Next, position your C-Thru ruler to intersect with the 35-degree mark and point C and mark a straight line in the upper arc. Repeat this step with the 45-, 55- and 65-degree markings to complete the shapes within the arc section, exactly as shown in the diagram.

20. Repeat Step 16 in the upper left-hand corner of the square. It may

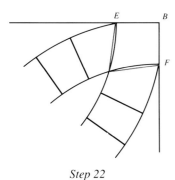

Step 22

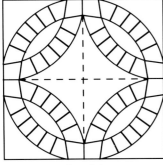

Step 24a

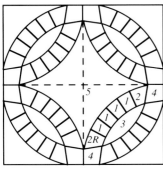

Step 24b

SUPPLIES:
Accurately drafted pattern
Template plastic
Red and black ultra-fine permanent
  pens
Large C-Thru ruler
Rotary cutter
Wide plastic ruler
Cutting board
Drafting tape
Artist's soft pencil, white, gray or
  silver
Sharp lead pencil
Fabric scissors
Glass-head pins
Fabric

be helpful to rotate your graph paper so that point A is in the lower right-hand corner.

21. Repeat Steps 17–19 to mark straight lines in the opposite arc section, placing the protractor at point A.

22. Notice that the line joining the post to the end of the pieced arc is curved. When sewing these two pieces together, the curves will be opposing and require some maneuvering to sew smoothly. You can easily avoid this situation if you will mark straight lines from the tip of the melon section to points E and F, exactly as shown in the diagram. Do this again at the opposite set of posts.

23. Use the eraser to eliminate the points made in Steps 17 and 21.

24. At this point you have drafted one-quarter of the ring and all of the shapes required to make the *Double Wedding Ring*. However, if you would like to draft the entire ring or view the entire pattern, you can repeat the previous steps three more times. Or you may choose to trace the block or make photocopies of it and tape the sections together to form the complete ring, exactly as shown in the diagram. Otherwise, this completes the *Double Wedding Ring*. There are five template shapes: #1 the inner segments of the pieced arc, #2 and 2R the ends of the pieced arc, #3 the melon shape, #4 the post and #5 the large background piece. Note that template shape #5 is only one quarter of the entire shape. To achieve the full shape the two straight sides must be placed on the fold when cutting the fabric shape. Indicate this on the template shape. *Do not* add seam allowance to these two sides when making your plastic template.

MAKING TEMPLATES FROM DRAFTED PATTERNS

Template patterns can now be made from your drafted patterns. These templates are used to trace the outline of the shape onto fabric for cutting individual pieces. The following information will be helpful in marking and cutting templates after you have completed the practice exercises and accurately drafted the patterns.

1. Mark a 1/4″ line for seam allowance around the outside of one of each template shape. For accuracy, place the large C-Thru ruler over the graph paper, lining up the 1/4″ mark on the ruler directly over the outline of the template shape, so that 1/4″ of the ruler extends beyond the marked line. Mark along the edge of the ruler with your red ultra-fine permanent pen.

2. Place the drafted pattern on your cutting board. Lay a piece of template plastic over the pattern and tape it in place around the edges.

3. With the template plastic placed over the drafted pattern, use the black ultra-fine permanent pen and large C-Thru ruler to mark the template shapes on the template plastic, following the red lines. Remove the graph paper from under the template plastic. Place the template plastic on the cutting board and tape it in place. Lay the edge of the wide plastic ruler directly over the marked line on the plastic. Use the rotary cutter to cut the templates apart, cutting just inside the line.

4. Use a permanent pen to write on each template: the block name, the template #, block size and direction of lengthwise grain.

5. Lay the plastic template on top of the wrong side of a single thickness of fabric. Make sure that the lengthwise marking on the template corresponds to the lengthwise grain of the fabric. Using the marking pencil, mark around the template.

6. Use your fabric scissors to cut the required number of fabric shapes from each fabric. If you are cutting multiple layers, pin the fabrics together inside the outline of the template pattern to keep the layers united and prevent them from slipping.

Now that you have worked through the practice exercises, you have the knowledge and experience to draft other pieced block patterns or to change block sizes as you desire. This will not only assist you in your everyday quiltmaking process but also be especially helpful with any of the pieced block patterns contained in this book. All of the pieced block patterns presented in Chapter Two have been given a grid category to make drafting these patterns in other sizes easier for you.

A CLASS OUTLINE

SUPPLIES:
8 sheets of graph paper, ⅛″ grid
Sharp lead pencil
C-Thru plastic 2″ × 18″ ruler (B-85)
Red ultra-fine permanent pen
Template plastic
Eraser
Compass
Protractor
Push pins
Cardboard, non-corrugated
Paper scissors
Fabric scissors
Rotary cutter
Wide plastic ruler
Cutting board
Artist's soft pencil, white, gray or
**   silver**
Sewing machine – OR –
Hand sewing needle
Cotton thread
Steam iron
Pressing surface
Light-colored towel

You will find this set of classes particularly useful at this point, since making this Drafted Sampler quilt provides immediate application of what has been learned about drafting.

Our block sizes have deliberately been omitted to encourage you to experiment. After the blocks have been accurately drafted and the individual template shapes marked with seam allowance, you can either make plastic templates or measure the shapes and use quick-cutting techniques for cutting the fabric shapes.

Six 3-hour classes

CLASS ONE: EASY BLOCKS: *Economy* and *Delectable Mountains*

In class: Draft *Economy* and *Delectable Mountains* blocks in any size. Cut fabric shapes for both blocks. Review the sew order diagrams in Chapter Two for both blocks.
Homework: Construct *Economy* and *Delectable Mountains* blocks.

CLASS TWO: INTERMEDIATE BLOCKS: *Kandy's Path* and *Indian Bonnets*

In class: Draft *Kandy's Path* and *Indian Bonnets* blocks in any size. Cut fabric shapes for both blocks. Review the sew order diagrams in Chapter Two for both blocks.
Homework: Construct *Kandy's Path* and *Indian Bonnets* blocks.

CLASS THREE: ADVANCED BLOCKS: *Dutch Rose* and *North Carolina Lily*

In class: Draft *Dutch Rose* and *North Carolina Lily* blocks in any size. Cut fabric shapes for both blocks. Review the sew order diagrams in Chapter Two for both blocks.
Homework: Construct *Dutch Rose* and *North Carolina Lily* blocks.

CLASS FOUR: CIRCULAR BLOCKS: *Fan* and *Double Wedding Ring*

In class: Draft *Fan* and *Double Wedding Ring* in any size. Make templates and cut fabric shapes for both blocks.

Homework: Construct *Fan* and *Double Wedding Ring* blocks. To square up the *Double Wedding Ring,* use the drafted quarter of template shape #5.

CLASS FIVE: SETTING, SASHING AND BORDERS

In class: Lay your sashing fabric, right side facing up, either on a flat surface or pinned to a design board. Place your blocks on the fabric in an attractive arrangement, using the sashing fabric as a unifying element; be sure to keep your blocks in straight horizontal and vertical lines, but feel free to vary the use and sizes of the sashing areas. Then, measure each of the sashing areas. Cut pieces of the required sizes, remembering to *add seam allowance to each piece.* Join the blocks to the sashing strips to form the quilt top. Add borders.

CLASS SIX: LAYER AND BASTE QUILTS

In class: Students help to baste all the quilts in preparation for quilting. Quilting demonstration.

Diana McClun

CHAPTER 2

PIECED QUILTS

SUPPLIES:
C-Thru plastic 2″ × 18″ ruler (B-85)
Wide plastic ruler
Cutting board
Right-angle triangle
Fabric scissors
Rotary cutter
Sewing machine with presser foot
  – OR –
Hand sewing needle
Masking tape (for use with sewing machine)
Cotton thread in a color to blend with your fabric, or neutral
Sharp lead pencil – OR –
Black ultra-fine permanent pen
Glass-head pins
Steam iron
Pressing surface
Light-colored towel

 If you ask what a quilt is, chances are a pieced quilt will be described to you. "Pieced quilt" and "quilt" are interchangeable in many people's minds. And pieced quilts are the essence of quiltmaking for most needleworkers.

During the second quarter of the nineteenth century, quiltmakers dramatically expanded their repertoire by creating literally thousands of pieced quilt block designs. By the turn of the twentieth century, thousands and thousands more had been created. A passion for pieced quilts continues unabated today.

Here, as in our first book, *QUILTS! QUILTS!! QUILTS!!!,* we have included pieced patterns that are simple and some that are more complex. We have included patterns that can be turned into quilts in a weekend and ones that may take months. In short, the beginner or the experienced quiltmaker will feel at home in this chapter.

We hope that you will alter or combine patterns included here. Look, for example, at Victoria Linn's quilt on page 62. She altered the traditional *Pine Tree* block, set her completed blocks together in a staggered arrangement, and renamed the pattern *Indian Bonnets.*

Using our templates, yardage charts and instructions, make one — or many — of the patterns offered here. Or, with the knowledge you acquired in Chapter One, re-draft any of the patterns, making them different sizes or altering some of their components. It's easy and it's fun.

And remember: any of the patterns in this chapter can be combined with appliqué, stencil work, crazy patchwork and trapunto. Look at the quilts on pages 55 and 126.

This chapter includes many favorite and frequently requested traditional quilt patterns. We have also included new patterns because we feel they are exciting designs and worthy of attention.

Each pattern includes the following:

1. A color photograph of an entire quilt, using the pattern.

2. A diagram of the individual pattern block which indicates the required templates (except for *Pineapple Log Cabin*).

3. *Complete instructions* for making the quilt, including quick-cutting techniques when appropriate.

4. Sew-order diagrams which indicate the order in which the individual pieces are sewn together.

5. Yardage requirements for a variety of bed and wall sizes.

6. Suggested fabrics.

7. Template patterns for each individual part of the pattern block. These templates can be used for both machine and hand work and are found on pages 166 to 191. (Templates are not required or given for *Pineapple Log Cabin*.)

8. A grid category so you can easily re-draft the pattern block in a larger — or smaller — size than we offer.

MAKING PIECED QUILTS

All levels of quiltmakers will require knowledge of the techniques described here in order to complete successfully the quilts included in this chapter. If you are an experienced quiltmaker, many of these techniques may already be familiar to you. However, if you are a beginner, you will want to review and practice the techniques carefully. Attempt them on old fabric before working with your quilt fabric.

Beginners will need to know:

1. How to achieve an accurate 1/4″ seam allowance. See "Things to Know About Your Sewing Machine Before Beginning to Sew."

2. Quick cutting techniques.

3. Proper pressing techniques.

4. How to attach borders (see pages 151 to 154).

If you also need help with fabric preparation, setting your blocks together, preparing to quilt or machine quilting, we suggest you consult our book *Quilts! Quilts!! Quilts!!! — The Complete Guide to Quiltmaking,* which details these skills for the beginner.

Beginners *and* experienced quiltmakers will need to know:

1. Strip piecing techniques

2. Making half-square triangles

3. Making double half-square triangles

4. Y-seam construction

THINGS TO KNOW ABOUT YOUR SEWING MACHINE BEFORE BEGINNING TO SEW

In quiltmaking, most sewing is done with a 1/4″ seam allowance. The seam allowance is the distance from the cut edge of the fabric to the line of stitching.

If you are planning to sew your quilt on the sewing machine, it will be necessary to make an accurate 1/4″ seam on the machine. To determine this distance, place your large C-Thru ruler under the presser foot and measure over 1/4″ to the right. Run a piece of masking tape at this point on the throat plate. ✳ *Helpful hint:* Several thicknesses of tape will prevent your fabric from going beyond that point.

QUICK CUTTING

Non-Directional Fabric

1. Place your fabric on your cutting board. Fold it in half lengthwise with the right side of the fabric facing you and the selvage edges even with each other. Then fold the fabric in half again lengthwise, bringing the folded edge even with the selvage edges. There are now four thicknesses.

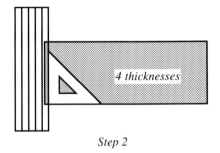

Step 2

2. Lay a right-angle triangle on top of the fabric, approximately 1/4″ away from the left-hand edge, with the bottom edge of the triangle even with the bottom fold of the fabric. (NOTE: Left-handed people reverse the placement.) Place the wide plastic ruler against the triangle, perpendicular to the folded edge. If you have a cutting board marked with lines, you can skip this step and line up the fabric with the lines on your board.

3. Remove the triangle and, with the rotary cutter, make a cut along the right edge of the ruler. Hold the cutter straight, not with the blade turned out, otherwise the cut edge will not be straight. Placing the weight of your free hand on the ruler, *push the cutter away from you with one strong motion, placing pressure into the board and keeping the blade tight against the ruler.* This will give a smoothly cut edge. *Do not make short, jerky cuts.*

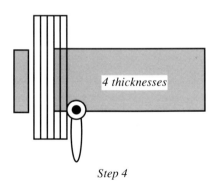

Step 4

4. Slide the ruler over to the right, so that the marking for the desired strip width on your ruler is even with the cut edge of the fabric. Run the rotary cutter along the right edge of the ruler, cutting off a strip of fabric. Unfold the strip and check to see that it is straight. ✳ *Helpful hint:* If there should happen to be a bend in the strip where the fabric was folded, you will need to refold your fabric; chances are that your selvage edges were not even to begin with.

Directional Fabric

Directional fabrics will give the best results if cut on the lengthwise grain. You will cut through only one thickness at a time, following the printed pattern, as you would otherwise not be able to see if underlying layers are being cut straight along the pattern. You should purchase no less than 5/8 yard if you are using a directional print. This will give you 22½″ (5/8 yard) along the lengthwise grain.

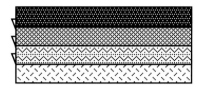

Step 2

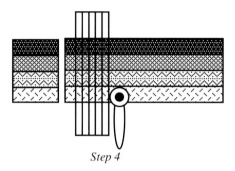

Step 4

STRIP PIECING

Rather than cutting individual template shapes, this quick technique allows you to sew cut strips together to form a set. Sets are then cut apart to form units of shapes. This technique can be a real time-saver.

1. Set the stitch length indicator on your machine to 8 to 10 stitches per inch (2.5 on some models). Thread your machine on the top and the bobbin with a cotton thread in a color to blend with your fabrics. A neutral is always good. *It is important to use the same type of thread in both the top and the bobbin to give the best results.*

2. Lay out the strips you have cut in the required sequence. Sew two strips right sides together along one of the 44″ sides. Be very careful not to pull or stretch the strips while sewing, as this may cause them to become wavy. Sew on any remaining strips in the proper sequence.

3. Press the set of strips. Refer to "Pressing" (which follows) for details.

4. With the right side of the fabric facing up, lay the pressed strips on the cutting board. Using the wide plastic ruler and rotary cutter, cut the strips at the width indicated by your quilt pattern. After a few cuttings you may need to re-align your cut edge with the ruler and board.

PRESSING

Pressing is an important step in quiltmaking. Get in the habit of pressing often. Keep your iron and pressing surface close at hand. Use a well-padded pressing surface, an ironing board or any level surface. A light-colored towel makes especially good padding, because it keeps any seam allowance from creating a ridge on the right side of your pieced fabrics.

We make a distinction between pressing and ironing. Pressing is an up-and-down motion; ironing involves pushing the fabric, which may stretch pieces out of shape.

Use a steam iron with the heat control set for cotton. The steam setting will apply a little moisture to the fabric and help eliminate any wrinkles. Keep the surface of the iron smooth and clean to avoid soiling the blocks.

After you have sewn a seam, press the fabrics flat to set the stitches in place. Fold the top piece of fabric back over the stitching line. Press. Seams pressed to one side are stronger than open seams. ✳ *Helpful hint:* If darker fabrics are on top, seams will automatically be turned in the direction of the darker fabric and will not shadow through under the lighter fabric. Make your pressed seams as sharp as possible.

HALF-SQUARE TRIANGLES

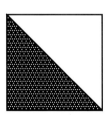

This unit, made from two right-angle triangles joined together along their longer sides to form a square, is commonly found in pieced quilt block patterns. There are many different quick methods for achieving this unit and we have included two of our favorites. The techniques can be used for making any size half-square triangle unit.

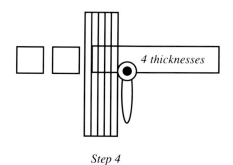

Step 4

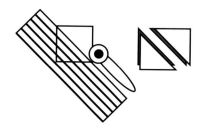

Step 5

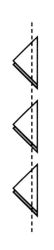

Step 6

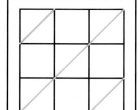

Step 3

Method One: Quick Cutting

1. With their right sides together and selvage edges even with each other, layer the two fabrics to be used for the half-square triangles. Since fabric widths vary, you may be able to align the selvage edges on only one side.

2. Fold the two fabrics in half lengthwise, with the wrong side of the fabric facing you and the selvage edges even with each other. There are now four thicknesses.

3. Using the methods of cutting described in Steps 2 through 4 of "Quick Cutting" above, cut the desired strip width.

4. Lay a pair of cut strips on the cutting board and, using the rotary cutter and wide plastic ruler, cut the strips to make squares.

5. Then cut each layer of squares in half diagonally to make triangles.

6. Take the stack of triangles to your sewing machine. The triangles are conveniently stacked alternately in color, right sides together, so you can simply pick them up in pairs and feed them through your machine. Sew the pairs together, exactly as shown in the diagram. ✷ *Helpful hint:* To save time do not break the chain of thread between the pairs.

7. With your scissors, clip the threads joining the pairs.

8. Use your scissors or rotary cutter and board to cut off the corners of the triangles, as pictured. With the darker fabric facing you, press the unit flat, then fold the darker triangle back over the stitching line. Press to form a square.

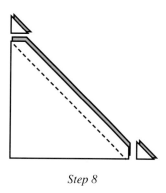

Step 8

Method Two: Grid

This quick-piecing technique was developed by Mary Ellen Hopkins.

1. Using your wide plastic ruler and rotary cutter, cut an 18" × 22" (or smaller, depending upon the number of units required) piece from each of two fabrics.

2. Using your ruler and a pencil or a black ultra-fine permanent pen, mark a grid of squares on the *wrong* side of the lighter fabric. The size of the grid will be 7/8" larger than the *finished* size of the half-square triangle.

3. Lightly mark diagonal lines in every other row of the grid, as indicated in the diagram.

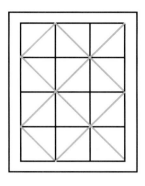

Step 4

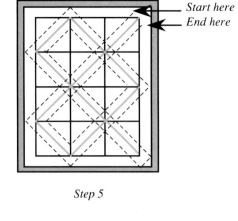

Start here
End here

Step 5

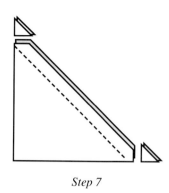

Step 7

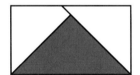

Step 1

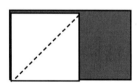

Step 2

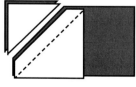

4. Next, lightly mark diagonal lines in the opposite direction in all of the empty squares.

5. With right sides together, place this marked fabric on top of the darker fabric. Lightly press the two layers together to remove any possible wrinkles. Place a few pins to hold the two layers in place. Starting in a corner which has a diagonal line going in towards the center of the grid, begin stitching 1/4″ to the left of the diagonal line, stopping to pivot at the corners and continuing around the grid until you have returned to the beginning. Every diagonal line will now have a 1/4″ stitching line on *both* sides.

6. Remove the pins. Press well. Lay the fabrics on the cutting board. Using your ruler and rotary cutter, cut through both thicknesses of fabric, cutting on *every* marked line (horizontal, vertical and diagonal). Or you may use fabric scissors.

7. Use your scissors or rotary cutter to cut off the corners of the triangles, as pictured. Press the unit flat, then fold the top triangle back over the stitching line. Press to form a square.

You will discover that each marked square on the grid made two half-square triangles. Therefore, if you have a grid of 4 squares across and 5 squares down (20 squares), you will end up with a total of 40 half-square triangles.

DOUBLE HALF-SQUARE TRIANGLES

This method allows you to sew three triangles together without cutting any triangles; you cut squares and rectangles.

1. With the right sides of the fabrics together, place one square piece on top of the rectangular piece. Stitch through both thicknesses diagonally across the square as shown. Be very careful to stitch from point to point in order to keep the angle sharp. ✱ *Helpful hint:* If you have difficulty stitching straight across the diagonal of the square, you can lightly press the square in half diagonally and then stitch along the fold, or lightly mark the diagonal with a pencil and then stitch along the marked line.

2. Press the triangle over the stitching line to check to see that the edges line up with those of the rectangle. If they do, use your fabric

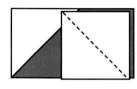

Step 3

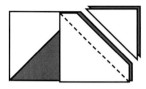

Step 4

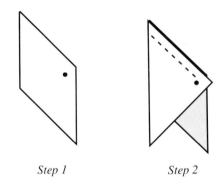

Step 1   *Step 2*

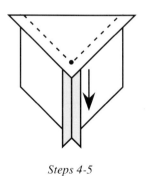

Steps 4-5

scissors or rotary cutter to trim the excess fabric to within 1/4" of the stitching line. If the edges do not line up perfectly when pressed, check to see that your stitching line is a true diagonal of your square.

3. Fold the resulting triangle over the stitching line and press. Take another square and place it on top of this unit as shown, then stitch across it diagonally.

4. Trim off the excess fabric to within 1/4" of the stitching line. Then proceed to fold and press as in Step 3. This completes the double half-square triangle unit.

To apply this quick technique to patterns which do not appear in this book, you must know the *finished* size of the unit. If you are unsure, draft the quilt pattern on graph paper and measure the length and width of one of its double half-square triangle units.

For the small triangles, cut squares the *finished* width of one unit *plus* 1/2". For the large triangle, cut a rectangle the *finished* width of the unit *plus* 1/2" × the *finished* length of the unit *plus* 1/2".

Y-SEAM CONSTRUCTION

Patterns which include joined diamonds often require this method to attach these diamonds successfully to other shapes, such as squares and triangles. Without using this simple technique, you will most probably create the inevitable pucker at the crook of the Y (the point where the three shapes meet).

1. Mark a point at the seam intersection on the wrong side of the diamonds, as indicated by the dot in the diagram.

2. With their right sides facing, sew one diamond to the other shape (triangle, square, etc.), starting at the dot and then stitching to the other end, exactly as shown in the diagram.

3. Place another diamond and the adjoining shape together, right sides facing.

4. Then stitch the adjoining shape to the diamond, *only up to the previous stitching line* at the crook of the Y.

5. With the right sides facing, stitch the two diamonds together, starting at the dot and stopping 1/4" from the end.

6. Press the Y leg seam open and the two Y arm seams down toward the diamonds.

This technique is also useful with other shapes which when joined form a Y.

LIBERTY COINS

Bernice Stone

Liberty Chinese Coins

Unit: $2'' \times 6''$
Techniques: Quick cutting and strip piecing or Template 2f
Fabric suggestions: Scraps for pieced rows. This example is a charm quilt; no two pieces are the same. (All fabrics are from Liberty of London.) Fabric for solid rows and borders to complement your pieced rows.

	Crib/Wall	Twin	Double/Queen	King
Finished size	$44'' \times 54''$	$68'' \times 90''$	$86'' \times 94''$	$104'' \times 94''$
Number of pieced double rows	2	3	4	5
Number of units per row	20	35	37	37
Number of solid rows	1	2	3	4

YARDAGE

	Crib/Wall	Twin	Double/Queen	King
Pieced rows: scraps to total	$1\frac{1}{8}$	$2\frac{3}{4}$	$3\frac{5}{8}$	$4\frac{1}{2}$
Solid rows and border	3	5	$5\frac{1}{4}$	$5\frac{1}{2}$
Backing	$3\frac{1}{4}$	$5\frac{1}{2}$	$8\frac{1}{4}$	$8\frac{1}{4}$
Binding	$\frac{5}{8}$	$\frac{3}{4}$	1	$1\frac{1}{4}$

CUTTING

	Crib/Wall	Twin	Double/Queen	King
Template 2f	80	210	296	370
— OR —				
Quick: see note below				
Solid rows, *each*	$6\frac{1}{2}'' \times 40\frac{1}{2}''$	$6\frac{1}{2}'' \times 70\frac{1}{2}''$	$6\frac{1}{2}'' \times 74\frac{1}{2}''$	$6\frac{1}{2}'' \times 74\frac{1}{2}''$
Border: width	$7\frac{1}{2}''$	$10\frac{1}{2}''$	$10\frac{1}{2}''$	$10\frac{1}{2}''$
Backing: number of lengths	2	2	3	3

Quick cutting: Cut all of your scrap fabrics into $2\frac{1}{2}'' \times 6\frac{1}{2}''$ rectangles.

CONSTRUCTION

1. Sew the required number of units together to form a single row as shown in the diagram.
2. Sew two rows together lengthwise to form a double row, as shown in the diagram.
3. Make the required number of double rows as indicated in the first chart.
4. Join the double rows lengthwise to the solid rows.

PINEAPPLE LOG CABIN

Kay Huston's method of making the quilt-as-you-go *Pineapple Log Cabin* was first featured in *Quilter's Newsletter Magazine* under the article "Teacher Tactics," September 1977. We wanted to share her innovative method of constructing this pattern because of its accuracy and speed.

Everything required to make this quilt is included in the book. However, if you wish to forego the process of tracing the entire pattern onto tracing paper, a full-size pattern can be purchased directly from Kay Huston at 185 West "G" Street, Benicia, CA 94510.

Block size: 15″
Techniques: Quick cutting, quilt-as-you-go (Template 12a)
Setting: Straight
Fabric suggestions: Eleven co-ordinated fabrics
Additional supplies: White tissue paper, iron-on transfer pencil, even-feed walking foot.

	Crib/Wall	Twin	Double	Queen	King
Finished size	55″ × 55″	65″ × 95″	81″ × 96″	89″ × 104″	104″ × 104″
Blocks set	3 × 3	3 × 5	4 × 5	4 × 5	5 × 5
# center blocks	1	3	6	6	9
# outside blocks	4	8	10	10	12
# corner blocks	4	4	4	4	4

YARDAGE

	Crib/Wall	Twin	Double	Queen	King
Muslin (for sewing guides)	2½	3¾	4½	4½	6
Fabric A	⅛	⅛	⅛	⅛	⅛
Fabric B	⅛	⅛	⅛	⅛	¼
Fabric C	⅞	1¼	2¼	2¼	2⅞
Fabric D	¾	1⅝	2⅛	2⅛	2⅞
Fabric E and inside border	1½	2¼	2¼	2¼	2⅜
Fabric F and binding	1	1½	1½	1½	1½
Fabric G	⅜	⅜	½	½	¾
Fabric H	⅜	⅜	½	½	¾
Fabric I	⅜	⅜	½	½	¾
Fabric J and middle border	(No middle border) ⅜	½	2¼	2⅜	2⅝
Fabric K and outside border	1¾	2½	2½	2¾	3⅛
Backing	3⅜	6⅛	7⅛	9½	11⅛
Batting	3½ yds. or 72″ × 90″ piece	6 yds. or 90″ × 108″ piece	7½ yds. or 90″ × 108″ piece	9 yds. or 120″ × 120″ piece	9 yds. or 120″ × 120″ piece

	Crib/Wall	Twin	Double	Queen	King
Muslin: number of 16″ squares	9	15	20	20	25
Inside border:					
Two for Sides A, *each*	2″×46″	5″×76″	2″×76″	2″×76″	2″×76″
Two for Sides B, *each*	2″×50″	5″×55″	2″×64″	2″×64″	2″×79″
Middle border:					
Two for Sides A, *each*	No middle border		4″×80″	6½″×80″	6½″×80″
Two for Sides B, *each*			4″×72″	6½″×77″	6½″×92″
Outside border:					
Two for Sides A, *each*	4″×50″	6″×86″	6″×88″	7½″×93″	7½″×93″
Two for Sides B, *each*	4″×60″	6″×67″	6″×84″	7½″×92″	7½″×108″
Backing: (see layout diagram)					
Two for Sides A, *each*	6″×49″	12″×76″	12″×76″	15″×76″	15″×76″
Two for Sides B, *each*	6″×60″	12″×67″	12″×84″	15″×92″	15″×108″
Number of 16½″ squares	9	15	20	20	25

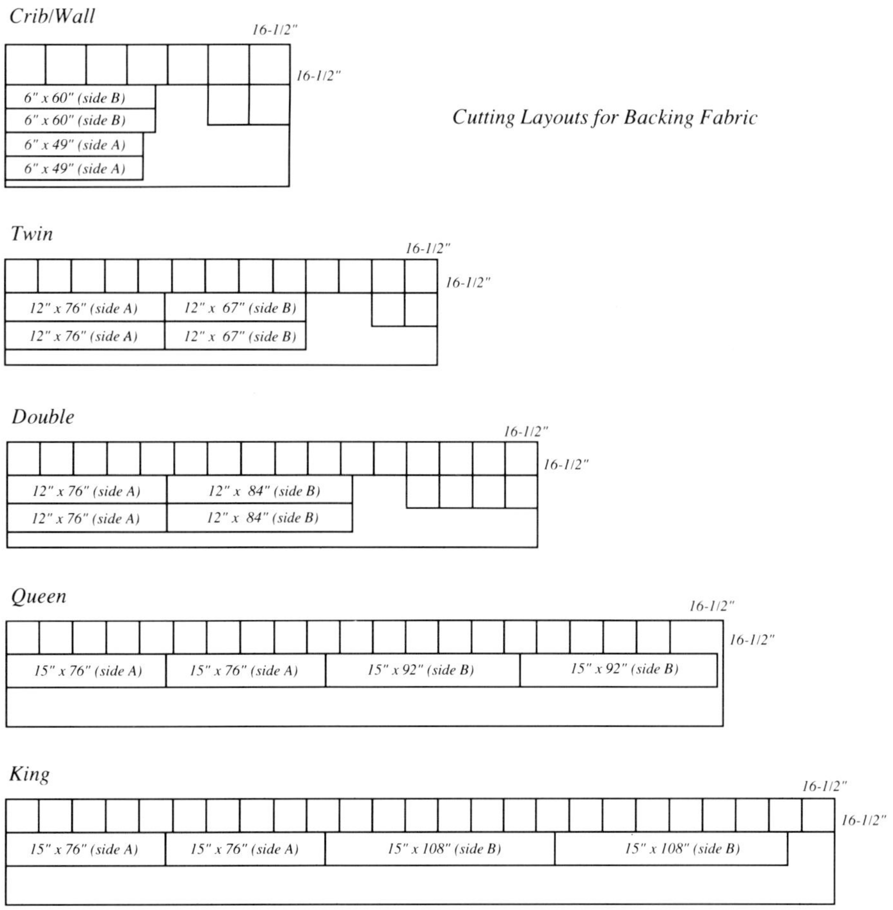

Crib/Wall

16-1/2″
16-1/2″

6″ x 60″ (side B)
6″ x 60″ (side B)
6″ x 49″ (side A)
6″ x 49″ (side A)

Cutting Layouts for Backing Fabric

Twin

16-1/2″
16-1/2″

12″ x 76″ (side A)   12″ x 67″ (side B)
12″ x 76″ (side A)   12″ x 67″ (side B)

Double

16-1/2″
16-1/2″

12″ x 76″ (side A)   12″ x 84″ (side B)
12″ x 76″ (side A)   12″ x 84″ (side B)

Queen

16-1/2″
16-1/2″

15″ x 76″ (side A)   15″ x 76″ (side A)   15″ x 92″ (side B)   15″ x 92″ (side B)

King

16-1/2″
16-1/2″

15″ x 76″ (side A)   15″ x 76″ (side A)   15″ x 108″ (side B)   15″ x 108″ (side B)

Batting: Lay a sewing guide on the batting and cut the same size for each block. Lay border strips of backing fabric on batting and cut the same size.

Quick cutting: Cut fabrics used for borders and binding lengthwise, cut all other fabrics crosswise.
- For Fabric A: Cut 2⅝"-wide strips. Then cut to 2⅝" squares.
- For Fabric B: Cut 1⅝"-wide strips.
- For Fabrics C, G, H, I and J: Cut 2"-wide strips.
- For Fabric D:

	Crib/Wall	Twin	Double	Queen	King
# of 2" strips	6	14	24	24	34
# of 3½" strips	2	5	7	7	9

- For Fabric E: Cut one 2⅝"-wide strip. Then cut to 2⅝" squares. Cut six 2"-wide strips.
- For Fabric K: Cut 3½"-wide strips.
- For Fabric F:

	Crib/Wall	Twin	Double	Queen	King
# of 1⅝" strips	3	4	5	5	6
# of 2" strips	3	4	5	5	6

PREPARATION

1. Place a piece of white tissue paper on a large, firm pressing surface.
2. With your iron set on cotton (no steam) press the tissue paper to shrink it.
3. Mark and cut a 16" square from the tissue paper.
4. Fold the tissue paper into quarters.
5. Lay one quarter of the tissue over Template 12a, lining up the centerpoint and quarter points of the tissue with those on the pattern.
6. Use your large C-Thru ruler and iron-on transfer pencil to trace the lines onto your tissue paper. Keep a pencil sharpener nearby to maintain a sharp point on the pencil. Press firmly to achieve a thin, accurate line.
7. Carefully rotate the tissue paper a one-quarter turn and trace the pattern again. One half of the pattern is complete.
8. Trace and rotate two more times to complete the block pattern on the tissue.
9. Place the tissue on a flat surface and, with the transfer pencil, mark a solid line ¼" beyond the outermost dotted lines all the way around.

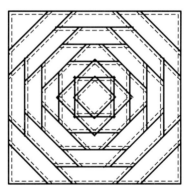

Steps 6-9

MAKING THE SEWING GUIDES

1. Lay one of the 16" squares of muslin on your pressing surface.
2. With the marked side down, lay the tissue pattern on top of the muslin. Secure in place with a few glass-head pins around the edges.
3. With your iron set on cotton (no steam) hold the iron in one place (for at least 10 seconds) on the tissue until lines appear on the muslin. Then move to another area and press. Continue pressing until all of the marked lines have been transferred to the muslin. ✱ *Helpful hint:* Lines transfer best when all thicknesses (pressing surface, towel and fabric) are hot.
4. Repeat Steps 1–3 with another 16" square of muslin. Several sewing guides can be made from one tracing on the tissue paper. When the lines become too faint, use the iron-on transfer pencil to re-trace the pattern onto the tissue paper.
5. Make the required number of sewing guides (muslin squares listed in cutting chart).

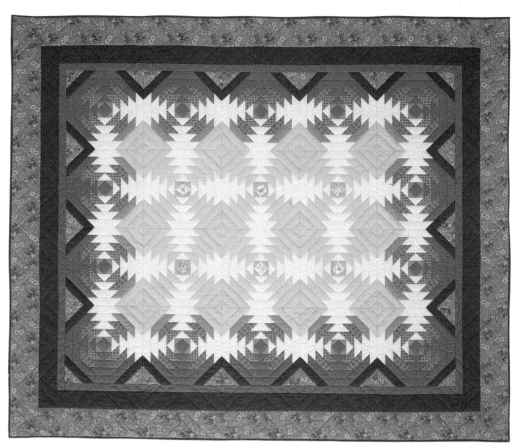

Kay Huston

Pineapple
Center Block

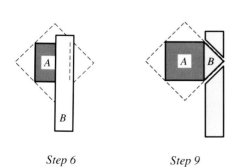

Step 6   *Step 9*

BLOCK CONSTRUCTION

Make the center blocks first.

1. With the wrong side facing up, place 16½″ square of backing fabric on a flat surface. Layer and center a 16″ square of batting and then a sewing guide (marked side up) on top of the backing fabric.

2. Secure the three layers with a few glass-head pins, pinning from the center of the block out to the edges.

3. With the right side facing up, place a 2⅝″ square of Fabric A on the center square of the sewing guide.

4. With their right sides together and raw edges even with each other on one side, place a strip of Fabric B on top of the Fabric A square. Secure with a pin.

5. Check your sewing machine for an accurate ¼″ seam allowance. Attach an even-feed walking foot to prevent puckering on the backing fabric, as you will be stitching through three layers. The stitching lines will show on the backing fabric, so be sure to use matching thread.

6. Pick up the layered unit and place it into the sewing machine. Beginning with a backstitch, stitch the Fabric B strip to the Fabric A square. End with a backstitch.

7. Cut threads on the top and the underside. Remove the block from the sewing machine.

8. Fold the Fabric B strip outward and finger press so the right side is facing up. The edge of the strip should meet the marked line on the sewing guide. If it does not, check to see that your seam allowance is an accurate ¼″.

9. Use your scissors to cut angles carefully on the strip to match those on the sewing guide.

10. Secure the cut strip in place with a pin.

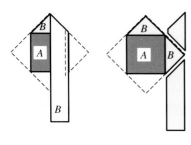

Step 12

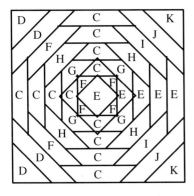

Step 19
Side Block

Step 20
Corner Block

11. Rotate the block one-quarter turn to the left.

12. Repeat Steps 4 through 10 for the next Fabric B angle.

13. Repeat two more times for the remaining Fabric B angles.

14. With their right sides together and their raw edges even with the marked line on the sewing guide, place a strip of Fabric C on top of the Fabric B strips.

15. Repeat the technique described in Steps 4–10 to attach strips of Fabric C and D, alternately, until you come to the corners. Start and stop ½" from the beginning and end on the last strip of Fabric D. It is necessary to leave this extra seam allowance loose for sewing two blocks together. Remember to keep the raw edge of the new fabric strip in line with the sewing guide, rather than the edge of the underlying fabric. This is because you may not have cut the angles exactly.

16. Hand tack the loose ½" seam allowance, stitching through only the Fabric D strip and the sewing guide. Do not stitch through the backing.

17. For the corner triangles, use a 3½" strip of Fabric D. Fold the backing out of the way. Stitch through the sewing guide and batting. After the blocks are joined, this section will be machine quilted.

18. Pin the backing fabric out of the way and, with your scissors, trim the batting and sewing guide even with the outermost line of the sewing guide.

19. Construct the side blocks, using the same method, substituting the appropriate fabric strips as shown in the diagram.

20. Construct the corner blocks, using the same method, substituting the appropriate fabric strips as shown in the diagram.

SEWING THE BLOCKS TOGETHER

1. Lay all the blocks on the floor in their proper order. It may be helpful to mark the horizontal rows 1, 2, 3, etc., with a piece of paper.

2. Pick up the first two blocks from the first row.

3. With their right sides together and raw edges even with each other, sew the two blocks together through their batting, sewing guide and fabric strip layers with a ¼" seam.

4. Attach the next block in the row in the same manner, keeping its backing loose. Repeat for any remaining blocks in the same row.

5. Turn the row of blocks to the back side. Trim some of the batting from the seam allowances.

6. Press the seam *open*, either by hand or gently with a steam iron. Be careful to press only on the seam and not to let the iron touch the batting, as it may melt the batting.

7. Use glass-head pins to secure the backing from one side of the block along the seam line which joins two blocks. Cut any excess backing which may extend beyond the seam line. You may need to cut V-shaped notches in the seam allowances where the seams meet the edge to eliminate bulk.

8. Fold the backing fabric from the adjoining block under itself only so that its folded edge is even with the center seam line. Secure to the blocks with glass-head pins.

9. Beginning and ending ½" from each end, hand slip stitch the folded edges of the backing fabric in place along the seam lines. This completes one horizontal row of blocks.

10. Repeat Steps 2 through 9 for the remaining horizontal rows.

11. Using the same technique described above for sewing blocks together, join the horizontal rows to each other with a ¼" seam. Press seams open and hand slip stitch the backing in place, remembering to begin and end the hand stitching ½" from each edge.

1. With the right side facing up, lay the quilt out on a flat surface.

2. With right sides together, and one edge even with the edge of the blocks, lay an inside Side A border strip along the left-hand side of the quilt.

3. Pin the border to the quilt through all layers. Check to see that the backing is smooth and without puckers.

4. Stitch the Side A border to the quilt along the length (through all layers) with a ⅛″ seam. This seam will simply hold the border in place while you attach the backing and batting strips. Trim any excess length from the border strip. Trim any excess backing and batting even with the edges of the quilt blocks.

5. Next, lay one of the Side A batting strips out on a flat surface.

6. With its right side facing up, and their lengthwise edges even with each other, lay a Side A backing strip on top of a Side A batting strip.

7. Next, with its right side facing up and their lengthwise left edges even with each other, lay the quilt top on top of the batting and backing strips.

8. Pin through all layers with glass-head pins along the left-hand edge.

9. Stitch through all layers with a ¼″ seam.

10. Repeat steps 1–9 for the other Side A inside border, batting and backing strips on the opposite side of the quilt.

11. With the right side facing up, open out all layers, so that the quilt is full width. Border strips will now be right sides facing up.

12. With the right sides together and one edge of the border strip even with the edge of the blocks, lay a Side B inside border strip along Side B of the quilt.

13. Pin the border to the quilt through all layers. The ends of the strip should meet the lengthwise edge of the previously attached Side A border strips. Trim any excess if necessary.

14. Stitch the Side B border strip to the quilt along the length with a ⅛″ seam.

15. Attach a Side B batting and backing strip as described in Steps 5–11 above. Note that the batting and backing strips will extend the entire width of the quilt.

16. Repeat Steps 12–15 for the other Side B inside border, batting and backing strips of the quilt.

17. With the right side facing up, lay the quilt out on a flat surface. All backing and batting strips should be extended flat and all four inside border strips right sides facing up.

18. With right sides together and lengthwise edges even with each other, lay a Side A middle border strip (outside border strip for crib/wall and twin) on top of one of the Side A inside border strips.

19. Pin the border to the quilt through all layers. The ends of the strip should meet the lengthwise edge of the previously attached Side B inside border strips. Trim any excess if necessary.

20. Stitch the border to the quilt with a ¼″ seam.

21. Repeat Steps 17–20 for the opposite side.

22. Attach all the outside border strips, alternately, using the same method described in Steps 17–20.

MELON PATCH

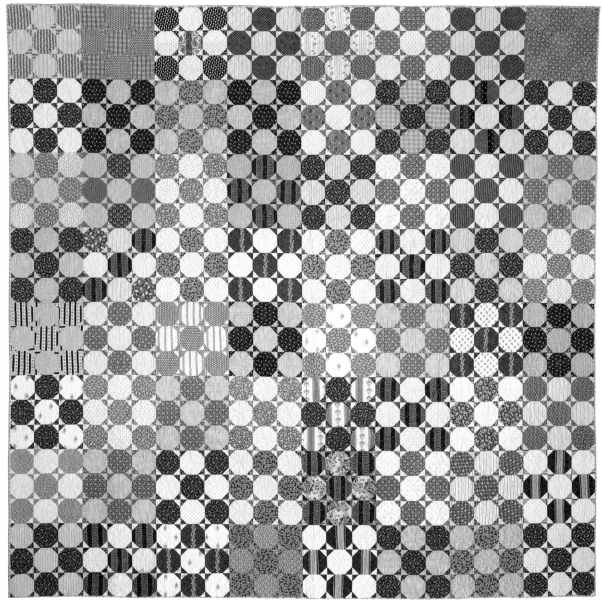

Maker unknown, c. 1875; collection of Diana McClun

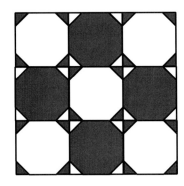

Block One

Block size: 12″
Grid category: Nine Patch
Techniques: Quick cutting or Templates 1r and 7a
Setting: Straight
Fabric suggestions: Variety of scraps

	Crib/Wall	Twin	Double	Queen	King
Finished size	36″×48″	60″×84″	84″×84″	84″×96″	108″×96″
Blocks set	3×4	5×7	7×7	7×8	9×8
Total blocks: one	6	18	25	28	36
Total blocks: two	6	17	24	28	36

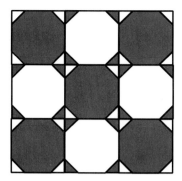

Block Two

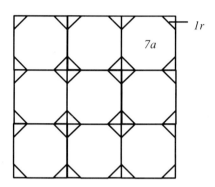

7a

1r

Step 1

YARDAGE

	Crib/Wall	Twin	Double	Queen	King
Light: scraps to total	1½	3½	4¾	5¼	6¾
Dark: scraps to total	1½	3½	4¾	5¼	6¾
Backing	1½	5	7½	8½	8½
Binding	⅝	1	1⅛	1⅛	1⅛

CUTTING

	Crib/Wall	Twin	Double	Queen	King
Template 1r: light and dark, *each*	216	628	884	992	1296
– OR –					
Quick: number of light and dark strips, *each*	8	24	32	36	47
Template 7a: light and dark, *each*	54	158	221	248	324
– OR –					
Quick: number of light and dark strips, *each*	6	18	25	28	36
Backing: number of lengths	1	2	3	3	3

Quick cutting: Cut all of your quilt top fabrics crossgrain.
   • For 1r: Cut 1½"-wide strips. Then cut to 1½" squares.
   • For 7a: Cut 4½"-wide strips. Then cut to 4½" squares.

CONSTRUCTION

   1. Using either traditional or quick methods, sew a Template 1r triangle of the opposite color to each corner of all 7a pieces, exactly as shown in the diagrams.
   2. Sew the units together, alternating light and dark to form blocks one and two, exactly as shown in the diagrams.
   3. Sew the blocks together, alternating blocks one and two, exactly as shown in the photo.

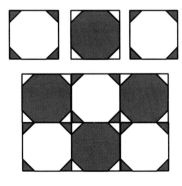

Block One

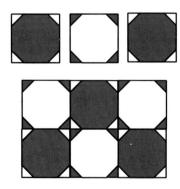

Block Two

KANDY'S PATH

Original design by Kandy Petersen, made by Laura Nownes and Diana McClun

Block size: 12″

Grid category: Four Patch

Techniques: Quick cutting, half-square triangles and double half-square triangles or Templates 3c, 2e, 4j, 1j, 2d

Setting: Straight

Fabric suggestions: Five fabrics for blocks. Border fabrics that complement your finished blocks.

	Crib/Wall	Twin	Double	Queen	King
Finished size	47″×47″	71″×95″	83″×95″	95″×95″	107″×95″
Blocks set	3×3	5×7	6×7	7×7	8×7
Total blocks	9	35	42	49	56

YARDAGE

	Crib/Wall	Twin	Double	Queen	King
For blocks:					
Blue	⅜	1⅛	1⅜	1½	1⅝
Brown	¾	2⅜	2⅝	3¼	3¾
Green	½	1⅜	1⅝	1⅞	2
Red	⅜	1⅛	1⅜	1½	1⅝
White	1	2½	2¾	3¼	3¾
For borders and corner blocks:					
Inside border	1⅛	2½	2½	2½	2¾
Outside border and binding	1⅛	2½	2½	2½	2¾
Backing	3	5¾	5¾	8½	8½

CUTTING

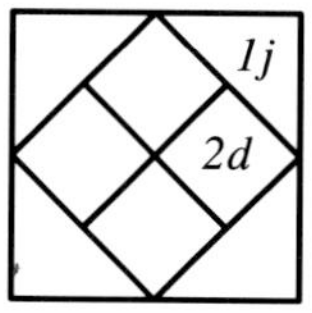

	Crib/Wall	Twin	Double	Queen	King
Blue					
Template 2d	54	210	252	294	336
– OR –					
Quick: number of strips	4	14	17	19	21
Brown					
Template 3c	144	560	672	784	896
– OR –					
Quick: number of 2½″ strips	5	18	21	25	28
and number of 2⅞″ strips*	3	10	12	14	16
Green					
Template 2e	36	140	168	196	224
– OR –					
Quick: number of strips	3	9	11	13	14
Red					
Template 2d	54	210	252	294	336
– OR –					
Quick: number of strips	4	14	17	19	21
White					
Template 4j	36	140	168	196	224
– OR –					
Quick: number of strips	3	9	11	13	14
Template 3c	72	280	336	392	448
– OR –					
Quick: number of strips*	3	10	12	14	16
Template 1j (corner blocks)	16	16	16	16	16

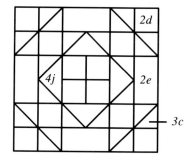

Corner Block

– OR –					
Quick: number of strips	1	1	1	1	1
Inside border fabric:					
border width:	2″	2″	2″	2″	2″
Template 2d (for corner blocks)	8	8	8	8	8
– OR –					
Quick: number of strips	1	1	1	1	1
Outside border fabric:					
border width:	4½″	4½″	4½″	4½″	4½″
Template 2d (for corner blocks)	8	8	8	8	8
– OR –					
Quick: number of strips	1	1	1	1	1
Backing: number of lengths	2	2	2	3	3

*Or use grid method for half-square triangles.

Quick cutting: Cut all of your quilt top fabrics (except borders) crossgrain.
- For 2d: Cut 2½″-wide strips. Then cut to 2½″ squares.
- For 2e and 4j: Cut 4½″-wide strips. Then cut to 2½″ × 4½″ rectangles.
- For 1j: Cut 3¾″-wide strips. Then cut to 3¾″ squares. Cut each square in *half diagonally.*
- For 3c: Brown: Cut the 2½″-wide strips to 2½″ squares.
     White: Cut 2⅞″-wide strips.
     Brown and white: Cut all the 2⅞″-wide strips to 2⅞″ squares. Cut each square in *half diagonally.*

CONSTRUCTION

Step 1

Step 2

1. For each block, make one unit, exactly as shown in the diagram.
2. For each block, make four double half-square triangle units, exactly as shown in the diagram. If using traditional methods, join the dark Template 3c triangles to the light Template 4j triangles or if using quick methods, join the dark 2½″ squares to the light 2½″ × 4½″ rectangles.
3. Join the brown and the white 3c triangles to make half-square triangle units.
4. Block sew order: see diagram.

Step 3

FLOWER GARDEN BASKET

Pieced by Coral Love and appliquéd by Diana McClun

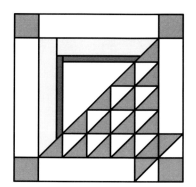

Block size: 14″

Grid category: Seven Patch

Techniques: Quick cutting or Templates 1o, 2d, 2g, 2h, 2j, 2k, 3c, 3k, 9b, 9c, 9d and 9e *and* Broderie Perse appliqué

Setting: Diagonal

Fabric suggestions: Light background and a variety of solids and prints for pieced blocks, chintz design fabric for cut-outs. Border fabric to complement your finished blocks.

	Crib/Wall	Twin	Double	Queen/King
Finished size	52″×52″	72″×91″	88″×88″	96″×96″
Blocks set	2×2	3×4	4×4	4×4
Total blocks	5	18	25	25
Total half blocks	4	10	12	12

YARDAGE

	Crib/Wall	Twin	Double	Queen/King
Light background	1½	2⅝	3¾	3¾
Solids and prints, scraps to total	1½	3¾	4⅜	4⅜
Design fabric	Yardage will vary with each fabric, depending upon the repeat. Purchase enough to obtain the required number of cut-out motifs.			
Border	1⅝	2¾	2¾	3
Backing	3¼	5½	7¾	8½
Binding	½	⅝	¾	1

CUTTING

	Crib/Wall	Twin	Double	Queen/King
Light background:				
Template 3c	10	36	50	50
– OR –				
Quick: number of strips*	1	2	2	2
Template 2g	10	36	50	50
– OR –				
Quick: number of strips	1	2	4	4
Template 3k	9	28	37	37
– OR –				
Quick: number of strips	1	3	4	4
Template 1o	4	4	4	4
– OR –				
Quick: number of strips	1	1	1	1
Template 2h	17	60	78	78
– OR –				
Quick: number of strips	2	4	5	5
Solids and prints:				
Template 3c	133	470	649	649
– OR –				
Quick: number of strips*	5	17	24	24
Template 2d	24	82	112	112
– OR –				
Quick: number of strips	2	6	7	7
Template 2k	9	28	37	37
– OR –				
Quick: number of strips	2	6	8	8
Template 2j	9	28	37	37
– OR –				
Quick: number of strips	2	6	8	8
Template 9b	4	4	4	4
– OR –				
Quick: number of strips	2	2	2	2
Template 9c	4	4	4	4
– OR –				
Quick: number of strips	1	1	1	1
Template 9e	9	28	37	37
– OR –				

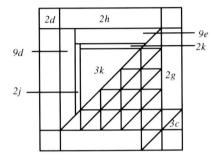

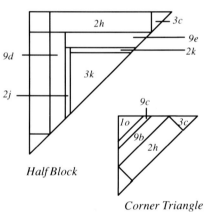

Half Block

Corner Triangle

Sew order for Block

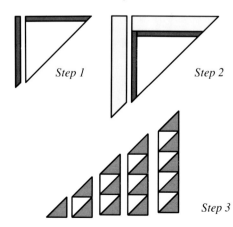

Step 1

Step 2

Step 3

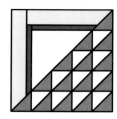

Step 4

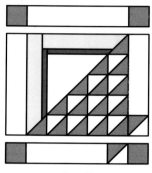

Step 5

Sew Order for Half Block

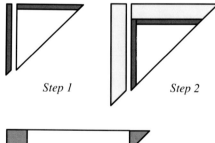

Step 1   *Step 2*

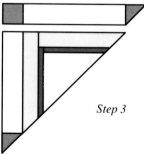

Step 3

Sew Order for Corner Triangle

Quick: number of strips	3	7	10	10
Template 9d	9	28	37	37
– OR –				
Quick: number of strips	1	2	2	2
Appliqué motifs	5	18	25	25
Border: width	6½″	6½″	6½″	8½″
Backing: number of lengths	2	2	3	3

*Or use the grid method for making half-square triangles

Quick cutting: Cut all of your quilt top fabrics (except borders) crossgrain.
- For 1o: Cut 5⅛″-wide strips. Then cut to 5⅛″ squares. Cut each square in *half diagonally.*
- For 2d: Cut 2½″-wide strips. Then cut to 2½″ squares.
- For 2g: Cut 8½″-wide strips. Then cut to 2½″ × 8½″ rectangles.
- For 2h: Cut 10½″-wide strips. Then cut to 2½″ × 10½″ rectangles.
- For 2j: Cut 1″-wide strips. Then use template to mark and cut angles.
- For 2k: Cut 1″-wide strips. Then use template to mark and cut angles.
- For 3c: Cut 2⅞″-wide strips. Then cut to 2⅞″ squares. Cut each square in *half diagonally.*
- For 3k: Cut 6⅞″-wide strips. Then cut to 6⅞″ squares. Cut each square in *half diagonally.*
- For 9b: Cut 2″-wide strips. Then use template to mark and cut angles.
- For 9c: Cut 1″-wide strips. Then use template to mark and cut angles.
- For 9d: Cut 2″-wide strips. Then use template to mark and cut angles.
- For 9e: Cut 2″-wide strips. Then use template to mark and cut angles.

CONSTRUCTION

1. Block sew order: see diagrams.
2. Half block sew order: see diagrams.
3. Corner triangle sew order: see diagram.
4. Appliqué a cut-out motif to each whole block.
5. Set the blocks together in a diagonal set, joining to the half blocks.

DELECTABLE MOUNTAINS

Made by Frances Gaddis Worley, c. 1850–1875, the great-great-grandmother of the owner, Margaret Petzel

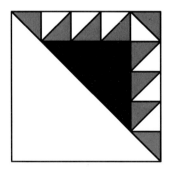

Block size: 5″
Grid category: Five Patch
Techniques: Quick cutting or Templates 1p, 1r, 3l
Setting: Diagonal
Fabric Suggestions: Light for background and two additional fabrics for pieced
   blocks. Border fabric that complements your finished blocks

NOTE: As you can see, the corners in the quilt pictured are not symmetrical. There is an extra row of half blocks at the bottom. Yardage and instructions are given leaving out this row so that the quilt will be symmetrical.

	Crib/Wall	Twin	Double	Queen	King
Finished size	50″ × 50″	71″ × 85″	80″ × 94″	87″ × 101″	106″ × 106″
Blocks set	6 × 6	9 × 11	10 × 12	11 × 13	14 × 14
Total blocks	60	178	218	262	364
Number of side triangles	16	32	36	40	48

	Crib/Wall	Twin	Double	Queen	King
Finished size	47″× 52″	69″× 86″	83″× 89″	93″× 89″	106″× 103″
Blocks set	3 × 2	4 × 3	5 × 3	6 × 3	8 × 4
Total number of blocks	8	18	23	28	53
Number of top and bottom triangles	4	6	8	10	14
Number of side pieces	2	4	4	4	6

YARDAGE

	Crib/Wall	Twin	Double	Queen	King
Background (includes first side borders)	1¼	2	2¼	2½	2¾
Green: scraps to total	1	2	2½	3	5½
Tree base fabric	¼	¼	⅜	⅜	⅝
Brown: scraps to total	½	1	1¼	1¼	1¾
Inside border	1¼	2	2	2¼	2⅝
Middle border	1½	2¼	2⅜	2⅜	3
Outside border and binding	1⅝	2½	2¾	2¾	3⅛
Backing	3	5	5¼	7¾	9

CUTTING

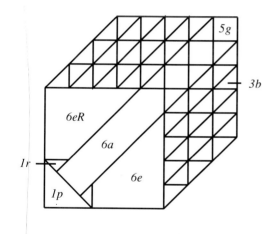

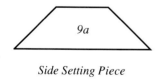

Side Setting Piece

	Crib/Wall	Twin	Double	Queen	King
Background:					
Narrow side borders: two strips *each* 1½″ ×	40″	62″	62″	62″	85″
Number of 11″ squares for top and bottom side triangles	1	2	2	3	4
Template 9a	2	4	4	4	6
Number of 6½″ squares for corner triangles	2	2	2	2	2
Template 5g	8	18	23	28	53
– OR –					
Quick: number of strips	1	1	2	2	3
Template 3b	64	144	184	224	424
– OR –					
Quick: number of strips	2	5	6	7	13
Template 6e	8 & 8R	18 & 18R	23 & 23R	28 & 28R	53 & 53R
Green scraps:					
Template 5g	16	36	46	56	106
– OR –					
Quick: number of strips	1	2	3	3	6
Template 3b	352	792	1012	1232	2332
– OR –					
Quick: number of strips*	11	24	30	37	69
Tree base fabric:					
Template 1p	8	18	23	28	53
– OR –					

Quick: number of strips	1	1	2	2	3
Brown scraps:					
Template 3b	16	36	46	56	106
– OR –					
Quick: number of strips	1	2	2	2	4
Template 6a	8	18	23	28	53
Template 1r	16	36	46	56	106
Inside border: width	1½"	3"	2½"	2½"	2½"
Middle border: width	2½"	4"	4½"	4½"	3½"
Outside border: width	4½"	7"	8½"	8½"	5½"
Backing: number of lengths	2	2	2	3	3

*Or use grid method for half-square triangles.

R = Reverse template on fabric.

Quick cutting: Cut all of your quilt top fabrics (except borders) crossgrain.
- For 5g: Cut 2"-wide strips. Then cut to 2" squares.
- For 3b: Cut 2⅜"-wide strips. Then cut to 2⅜" squares. Cut each square in *half diagonally.*
- For 1r: Cut 1⅞"-wide strips. Then cut to 1⅞" squares. Cut each square in *half diagonally.*
- For 1p: Cut 3⅞"-wide strips. Then cut to 3⅞" squares. Cut each square in *half diagonally.*
- For top and bottom side triangles: Cut each 11" square into *quarters diagonally.*
- For corner triangles: Cut both 6½" squares in *half diagonally.*

NOTE: The side and corner triangles were cut too big. They can be trimmed off after the blocks are set together.

CONSTRUCTION

1. Sew order: see diagram.
2. Set blocks together, joining to side pieces and side triangles, exactly as shown in the diagram.

Step 1

Step 2

DOUBLE WEDDING RING

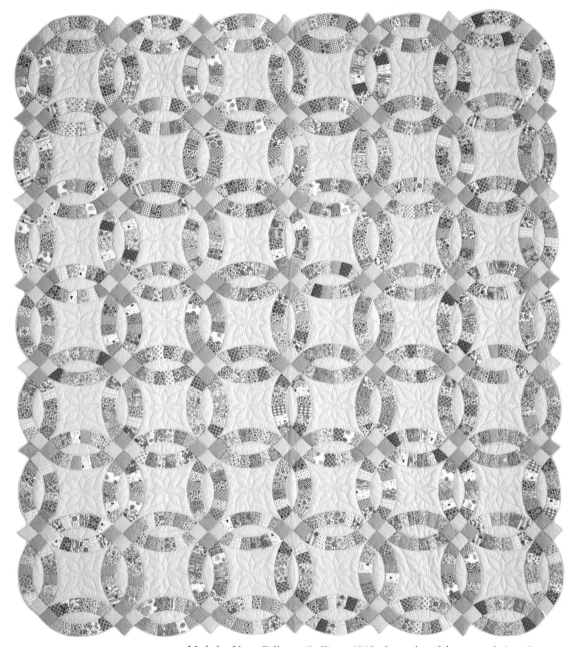

Made by Verna Folkman Stallings, 1949, the mother of the owner, JoAnn Sontag

17″ ring
Grid category: Circular
Techniques: Templates 10a, 10b, 10c, 10d and 10e
Fabric suggestions: Light background, scraps for rings.

	Crib/Wall	Twin	Double	Queen	King
Finished size	41″ × 54″	79″ × 90″	90″ × 90″	90″ × 94″	94″ × 94″
Rings set	3 × 4	6 × 7	7 × 7	7 × 8	8 × 8
# Rings with 4 melon units	1	1	1	1	1
# Rings with 3 melon units	5	11	12	13	14
# Rings with 2 melon units	6	30	36	42	49

YARDAGE

	Crib/Wall	Twin	Double	Queen	King
Background, posts and binding (bias)	3½	6½	7½	8½	9½
Rings: scraps to total	1¾	4¾	5½	6¼	7
Posts (second color):	¼	¾	⅞	1	1⅛
Backing	1⅝	5½	8	8¼	8¼

CUTTING

	Crib/Wall	Twin	Double	Queen	King
Background fabric:					
Template 10a	12	42	49	56	64
Template 10b	31	97	112	127	144
Template 10c	36	108	126	149	156
Ring fabrics:					
Template 10d	62 and 62R*	194 and 194R	224 and 224R	254 and 254R	288 and 288R
Template 10e	248	776	896	1006	1152
Posts (second color):					
Template 10c	36	108	126	149	156
Backing: number of lengths	1	2	3	3	3

*R = reverse template on fabric.

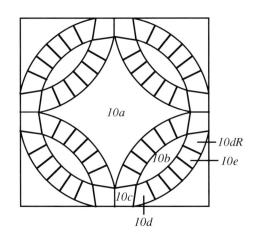

10a
10dR
10e
10b
10c
10d

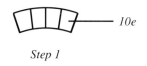

10e

Step 1

10d
10dR

Step 2

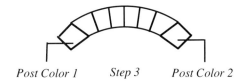

Post Color 1
Step 3
Post Color 2

CONSTRUCTION

1. Sew four shape 10e pieces together for each arc unit, exactly as shown in the diagram. ✳ *Helpful hint:* Chain units in pairs.

2. Attach a shape 10d and 10dR to each arc unit, exactly as shown in the diagram.

3. Sew a post of each color to one-half of the total number of arc units, exactly as shown in the diagram.

4. Carefully press all seams to one direction, being careful not to stretch the units.

5. Transfer the centerpoint markings and dots from Templates 10a, 10b and 10c onto the wrong side of each appropriate fabric shape.

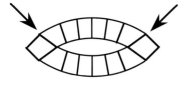

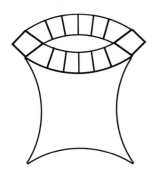

Step 10

Steps 13-14

6. With their right sides together, pin a pieced arc unit without posts to a melon shape (Template 10b). Match the centerpoints. The dots on the melon should line up with the seam joining shape 10d to shape 10c. Secure with pins at these points.

7. With the arc unit on top, stitch the shapes together, starting and stopping at the dots.

8. Press the seam toward the melon.

9. Using the same technique of matching centerpoints, pin and then sew the remaining arc units with posts to the opposite side of the melon units. Be sure to stitch with the melon on top, starting and stopping at the dots.

10. Stitch the post on each end to the adjoining end piece, stitching in the direction of the arrow, up to the previous stitches at the dot. This completes the melon/arc unit, as shown in the diagram.

11. Press the seam toward the melon.

12. With their right sides together, pin a melon/arc unit to one side of shape 10a. Match and secure their centerpoints with a pin. Place a pin at each of the other seams along the pieced arc.

13. With the background shape on top, stitch the shapes together, starting and stopping at the dots.

14. Press the seam toward the background fabric.

15. Attach additional melon/arc units as needed to each background shape. Refer to the chart above for the number of melon units per ring.

16. Arrange your rings exactly as shown in the diagram.

17. Join the rings in horizontal rows, exactly as shown in the diagram.

18. Join the horizontal rows together to complete the quilt top, exactly as shown in the diagram. It will be necessary to start and stop at the intersection of each post unit.

Step 16

Step 17

Step 18

TRIPLE STAR / SAWTOOTH STAR

Alex Anderson

Original setting by Alex Anderson

Block size: 12″ (Triple Star); 6″ (Sawtooth Star)
Grid Category: Four Patch
Techniques: Quick cutting and double half-square triangles or Templates 1e, 1m, 1r, 2d, 3b, 3c, 4b, 4c, 4f, 4k, 5d, 5g *and* Templates 6b and 7f
Setting: Straight
Fabric suggestions: Variety of light, medium and dark fabrics.

	Crib/Wall
Finished size	56″ × 56″
Total Triple Star blocks	9
Total Sawtooth Star blocks	28

YARDAGE

	Crib/Wall
Scraps to total	5½
Backing	3½
Binding	⅜

CUTTING

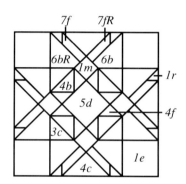

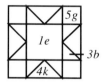

	Crib/Wall
Triple Stars:	
Template 4c	36
— OR —	
Quick: number of strips	2
Template 1e	36
— OR —	
Quick: number of strips	2
Template 1r	72
— OR —	
Quick: number of strips	2
Template 4f	72
— OR —	
Quick: number of strips	4
Template 7f	36 & 36R*
— OR —	
Quick: number of strips	6
Template 6b	36 & 36R
— OR —	
Quick: number of strips	4
Template 3c	36
— OR —	
Quick: number of strips	2
Template 4b	36
— OR —	
Quick: number of strips	2
Template 1m	36
— OR —	
Quick: number of strips	2
Template 5d	9
— OR —	
Quick: number of strips	1
Sawtooth Stars:	
Template 1e	28
— OR —	
Quick: number of strips	3

Template 3b	224
_– OR –_	
Quick: number of strips	11
Template 4k	112
_– OR –_	
Quick: number of strips	6
Template 5g	112
_– OR –_	
Quick: number of strips	6
Pieced border:	
Template 2d	12
_– OR –_	
Quick: number of strips	1
Template 3c, light and dark, _each_	196
_– OR –_	
Quick: number of light and dark strips, _each_	7
Backing: number of lengths	2

*R = Reverse template on fabric.

Quick cutting: Cut all of your quilt top fabrics (except borders) crossgrain.
- For 5d: Cut 3¼″-wide strips. Then cut to 3¼″ squares.
- For 4f: Cut 1⅞″-wide strips. Then cut to 1⅞″ squares.
- For 4b: Cut 3¼″-wide strips. Then cut to 1⅞″ × 3¼″ rectangles.
- For 3c: Cut 2⅞″-wide strips. Then cut to 2⅞″ squares. Cut each square in _half diagonally._
- For 1m: Cut 2″-wide strips. Then cut to 2″ squares.
- For 7f and 7fR: Cut 1¼″-wide strips. Then use template to mark and cut angles.
- For 6b and 6bR: Cut 3⅞″-wide strips. Then cut to 3⅞″ squares. Cut each square in _half diagonally._ Use template to mark and cut angle.
- For 4c: Cut 5¼″-wide strips. Then cut to 5¼″ squares. Cut each square into _quarters diagonally._
- For 1e: Cut 3½″-wide strips. Then cut to 3½″ squares.
- For 3b: Cut 2″-wide strips. Then cut to 2″ squares.
- For 4k: Cut 3½″-wide strips. Then cut to 2″ × 3½″ rectangles.
- For 2d: Cut 2½″-wide strips. Then cut to 2½″ squares.
- For 1r: Cut 2″-wide strips. Then cut to 2″ squares. Cut each square in _half diagonally._
- For 5g: Cut 2″-wide strips. Then cut to 2″ squares.

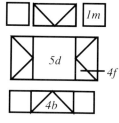

Step 2

CONSTRUCTION

Triple Stars

If quick-cutting and piecing techniques are used, the center star of the *Triple Star* will be slightly (approximately 1/16″) too small. However, it can easily be made to fit.

1. Make double half-square triangle units using Template pieces 4f and 4b.
2. Complete the center star exactly as shown in the diagram.
3. Sew order: see diagram.

✷ *Helpful hint:* Note how the edges overhang when joining Templates 1r and 7f, exactly as shown in the diagram.

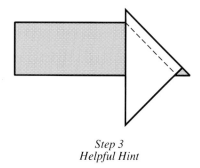

Step 3
Helpful Hint

Sawtooth Stars

1. Make double half-square triangle units using Template pieces 3b and 4k.
2. Sew order: see diagram.

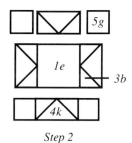

Step 2

Pieced Border

1. Make half-square triangle units using the light and dark Template 3c pieces.
2. Sew order: see diagram.

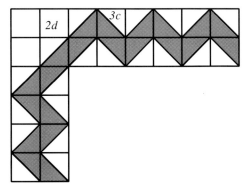

Step 2
Pieced Border

DUTCH ROSE

Made by Sarah Jane Small Gray; collection of Rae Davis Felthouse, a descendant

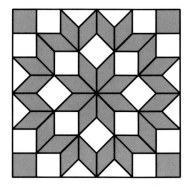

Block size: 12"
Grid category: Eight-Pointed Star
Techniques: Quick cutting or Templates 1c, 3g, 4e, 2m and 2n
Setting: Diagonal
Fabric suggestions: Two contrasting colors: light and medium or light and dark. Solids or prints or combination of the two.

	Crib/Wall	Twin	Double/Queen	King
Finished size	65"×65"	65"×86"	86"×86"	108"×108"
Blocks set	2×2	2×3	3×3	4×4
Total blocks	12	17	24	40
Total half blocks	12	14	16	20

YARDAGE

	Crib/Wall	Twin	Double/Queen	King
Light background (includes binding)	3⅜	4¼	5	8¼
Pink	2¼	3	3¾	5¾
Backing	4	5	7½	9½

CUTTING

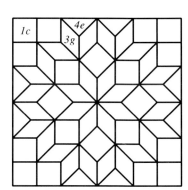

	Crib/Wall	Twin	Double/Queen	King
Light background:				
Template 1c	276	370	496	780
– OR –				
Quick: number of strips	16	21	28	44
Template 4e	168	220	288	440
– OR –				
Quick: number of strips	4	5	7	10
Sashing: number of 3¾" × 12½" pieces	36	48	64	100
Posts: number of 3¾" squares	13	18	25	18
Side posts: number of 5⅞" squares	2	3	3	4
Corner posts: number of 3¼" squares	2	2	2	2
Pink:				
Template 3g	576	768	1024	1600
– OR –				
Quick: number of strips	36	48	64	100
Template 1c	72	96	128	200
– OR –				
Quick: number of strips	4	6	8	12

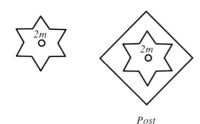

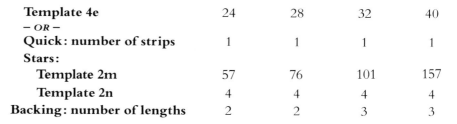

Template 4e	24	28	32	40
– OR –				
Quick: number of strips	1	1	1	1
Stars:				
Template 2m	57	76	101	157
Template 2n	4	4	4	4
Backing: number of lengths	2	2	3	3

Post

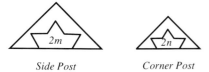

Quick cutting: Cut all of your quilt top fabrics crossgrain.
- For 3g: Cut 1¾″-wide strips. Then use template to mark and cut angles.
- For 1c: Cut 2¼″-wide strips. Then cut to 2¼″ squares.
- For 4e: Cut 3¾″-wide strips. Then cut to 3¾″ squares. Cut each square into *quarters diagonally.*
- For side posts: Cut each 5⅞″ square into *quarters diagonally.*
- For corner posts: Cut both 3¼″ squares in *half diagonally.*

Side Post   *Corner Post*

CONSTRUCTION

This block requires accurate piecing to be successful and lie flat. Use Y-seam construction.

1. For each whole block make 16 units, exactly as shown in the diagram.
2. Block sew order: see diagrams.
3. Make the required number of half blocks.
4. Use the paper basting method of appliqué to attach a star to each post, side post and corner post. After securing the star points, remove the paper pattern, mark and then cut the small center circle. Carefully turn the edges under and hand stitch. NOTE: Only a portion of the star is required for the side and corner posts. Position the stars as shown in the diagrams, trim and then stitch.
5. Appliqué a star at the center of each sashing strip.
6. Join the blocks to the sashing strips in a diagonal set.

Step 1

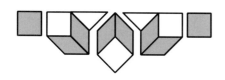

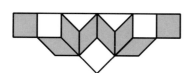

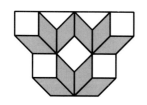

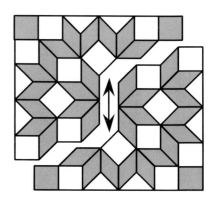

Step 2

NORTH CAROLINA LILY

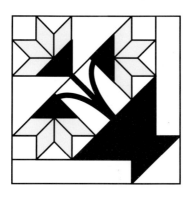

Block size: 12″
Grid category: Eight–Pointed Star
Techniques: Quick cutting or Templates 1c, 1o, 3d, 3g, 3k, 3n, 4e, 5h, 5j, 5k and 8a, appliqué and Y-seam construction
Setting: Straight
Fabric suggestions: One light, one medium and one dark

	Crib/Wall	Twin	Double/Queen	King
Finished size	30″ × 30″	62″ × 88″	88″ × 88″	114″ × 114″
Blocks set	2 × 2	4 × 6	6 × 6	8 × 8
Total blocks	4	24	36	64

YARDAGE

	Crib/Wall	Twin	Double/Queen	King
Light background	1½	5	7¾	9
Medium (including binding)	1	2½	3	4¾
Dark	¾	1½	2⅛	3⅛
Backing	1¼	5¼	7¾	10

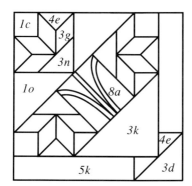

CUTTING

	Crib/Wall	Twin	Double/Queen	King
Light background:				
Inside border:				
Two for sides A at:	3″ × 21″	3″ × 74″	3″ × 74″	3″ × 100½″
Two for sides B at:	3″ × 21″	3″ × 47½″	3″ × 74″	3″ × 100½″
Sashing one	—	6	8	12
Sashing two	—	1	4	12
Template 4e	52	196	276	464
– OR –				
Quick: number of strips	2	5	7	11
Template 1c	16	76	112	196
– OR –				
Quick: number of strips	2	4	6	11
Template 1o	8	48	72	128
– OR –				
Quick: number of strips	1	3	5	8
Template 8a	4	24	36	64
– OR –				
Quick: number of strips	1	3	4	7
Template 5k	8	48	72	128
– OR –				
Quick: number of strips	1	3	4	8
Template 3d	4	24	36	64

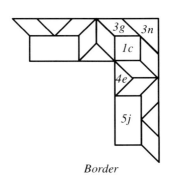

Border

Pieced by Jan Snelling and Mary K. Ryan and quilted by Cindy Gates and The Delectable Mountain Quilters and Martha Ochmanski. Commissioned by the Vermont Quilt Festival. Collection of Peggy Moran.

— OR —				
Quick: number of strips	1	2	2	4
Template 5j	4	4	4	4
— OR —				
Quick: number of strips	1	1	1	1
Medium:				
Template 3g*	112	400	560	936
— OR —				
Quick: number of strips	9	31	44	72
Dark:				
Template 3g*	32	80	96	136
— OR —				
Quick: number of strips	3	7	8	11
Template 3n	20	80	116	200
— OR —				
Quick: number of strips	1	4	5	9
Template 4e	8	48	72	128
— OR —				
Quick: number of strips	1	2	2	3

Stems: yards (¼" wide)	2	10	15	27
Template 3k	4	24	36	64
– OR –				
Quick: number of strips	1	2	3	6
Backing: number of lengths	1	2	3	3

*If you are using directional fabric, cut one half of shapes with the template reversed on the fabric.

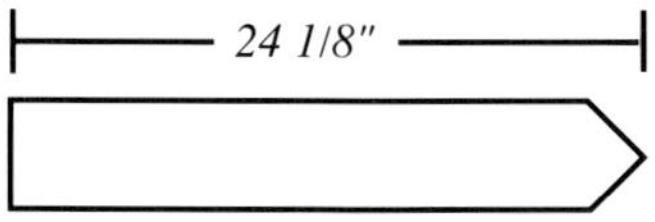

Quick cutting: Cut all of your quilt top fabrics (except borders) crossgrain.
- For 3g: Cut 1¾"-wide strips. Then use template to mark and cut angles.
- For 3n: Cut 3⅜"-wide strips. Then cut to 3⅜" squares. Cut each square in *half diagonally.*
- For 4e: Cut 3¾"-wide strips. Then cut to 3¾" squares. Cut each square into *quarters diagonally.*
- For 1c: Cut 2¼"-wide strips. Then cut to 2¼" squares.
- For 1o: Cut 5⅛"-wide strips. Then cut to 5⅛" squares. Cut each square in *half diagonally.*
- For 8a: Cut 4¾"-wide strips. Then cut to 4" × 4¾" rectangles.
- For 3k: Cut 6⅞"-wide strips. Then cut to 6⅞" squares. Cut each square in *half diagonally.*
- For 5k: Cut 9"-wide strips. Then cut to 2¼" × 9" rectangles.
- For 3d: Cut 4⅜"-wide strips. Then cut to 4⅜" squares. Cut each square in *half diagonally.*
- For 5j: Cut 4"-wide strips. Then cut to 2¼" × 4" rectangles.
- For sashing one: Cut 3" × 24⅛" rectangles. Then use angle guide template 5h to mark and cut angles, exactly as shown in the diagram.
- For sashing two: Cut 3" × 23¾" rectangles. Then use angle guide template 5h to mark and cut angles, exactly as shown in the diagram.
- For stems: Use one of the methods for making ¼"-wide finished bias strips. See Chapter Three.

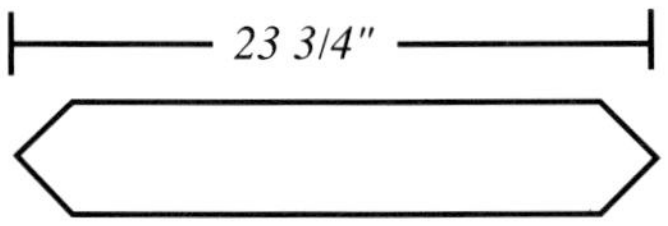

Sashing 1

Sashing 2

CONSTRUCTION

This block requires accurate piecing to be successful and lie flat. Y-seam construction is used in sewing the diamonds to the squares and triangles.

1. Sew the Template 3g medium-colored diamonds for the lilies together in pairs, exactly as shown in the diagram.

2. Join the pairs together to make lily units, exactly as shown in the diagram. Make 12 units for Crib/Wall; 72 units for Twin; 108 units for Double/Queen and 192 units for King.

3. Sew a Template 3n dark triangle to each unit, exactly as shown in the diagram.

4. Sew two light Template 4e triangles and one Template 1c light square to each lily unit, exactly as shown in the diagram.

Make the following:

	Crib/Wall	Twin	Double/Queen	King
Unit A	4	24	36	64
Unit B	4	24	36	64
Unit C	4	24	36	64

5. Sew a light Template 1o triangle to each side of the Unit A lilies, exactly as shown in the diagram.

6. Stems: Use one of the methods for making stems described in Chapter Three. The finished width of the stem is 1/4".

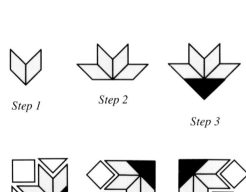

Step 1   *Step 2*   *Step 3*

Unit A   *Unit B*   *Unit C*

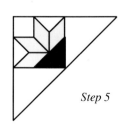

Step 5

Step 8

7. Position the stem pieces onto the Template 8a rectangle and appliqué in place.

8. Sew a Unit B and Unit C lily to each stem section, exactly as shown in the diagram.

9. Sew the Unit A lily section to the stem section, exactly as shown in the diagram.

10. Sew a Template 3k dark triangle to each unit, exactly as shown in the diagram.

11. Sew a Template 4e dark triangle to each Template 5k rectangle. NOTE: One half are sewn on the right-hand side and one half are sewn on the left-hand side, exactly as shown in the diagram.

12. Sew order to complete block: see diagram.

13. Join four blocks together, exactly as shown in the diagram.

Step 9-10

Step 11

Step 12

Step 13

Step 1

Sashing and Setting

1. Sew medium-colored diamonds to the angled ends of each sashing strip. Then sew the sides of the diamonds to each other.

2. Assembly: see diagram.

Step 2

Borders

Mary Ryan indicates that adjustment points were required to make the pieced borders fit. In most cases the border will be slightly too long. Make a few adjustments in the seams joining two diamonds. (The border shown on the quilt in the photo would require too much adjusting for the Crib/Wall size quilt and for this reason a suggested border for this size only is shown below.)

1. Make lily units, exactly as shown in the diagram.

2. Sew two Template 4e triangles to each lily unit, exactly as shown in the diagram.

3. Join the required number of lily units together for each border strip, referring to the chart below. Then inset Template 5j .

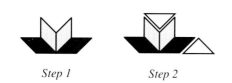

Step 1   *Step 2*

	C/W	T	D/Q	K
Number of lily units for each side A	5	12	12	16
Number of lily units for each side B	5	8	12	16

4. Add a Template 4e triangle to each pieced strip, exactly as shown in the diagram.

5. For a Crib/Wall size quilt, join the border strips to the quilt top, then add a Template 1c square and then a 3n triangle to each corner, exactly as shown in the diagram. For all other sizes proceed as follows:

6. Use Y-seam construction to make eight inside corner units, exactly as shown in the diagram.

7. Add a Template 1c square to four of these units, exactly as shown in the diagram.

8. Make eight outside corner units, exactly as shown in the diagram.

9. Join the inside border strips to the pieced border strips and corner units, adding two Template 5j rectangles at each corner, exactly as shown in the diagram.

10. Join the border strips to the quilt top.

11. Stitch the corner stars together diagonally. Then attach a Template 3n triangle to each corner, exactly as shown in the diagram.

Step 3-4

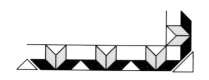

Step 5

Step 6   *Step 7*   *Step 8*

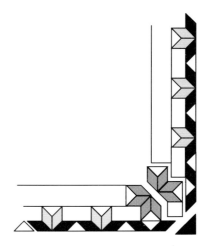

Steps 9-11

FEATHERED STAR

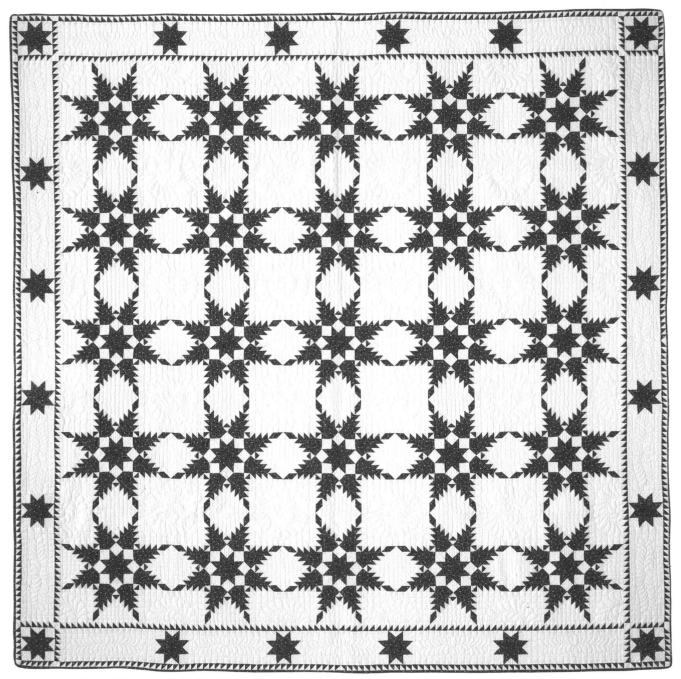

Mary K. Ryan, Jan Snelling and Merial Liberty. Commissioned by the Vermont Quilt Festival. Collection of Martha Barclay.

Block size: 16⅛″
Techniques: Quick cutting or Templates 1a, 1b, 1h, 1m, 3a, 3f, 3h, 3j, 4a, 4f, 4h, 4l and 6d
Setting: Straight
Fabric suggestions: Light and dark

	Wall	Crib	Twin	Double/Queen	King
Finished size	29″ × 29″	45″ × 61″	77″ × 93″	93″ × 93″	109″ × 109″
Blocks set	1	2 × 3	4 × 5	5 × 5	6 × 6
Total blocks	1	6	20	25	36
# Border stars	4	10	18	20	24

YARDAGE

	Wall	Crib	Twin	Double/Queen	King
Dark	1	2⅛	5	6	8
Light	1½	3	6¼	7¾	10¼
Backing	1	3¾	5½	8¼	9½
Binding	½	½	¾	⅞	1

CUTTING

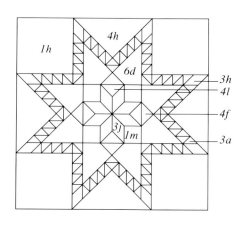

	Wall	Crib	Twin	Double/Queen	King
Dark:					
Template 3j	8	48	160	200	288
— OR —					
Quick: number of strips	1	3	10	12	17
Template 3a	296	776	1992	2344	3104
— OR —					
Quick: number of strips*	6	17	42	49	65
Template 3h	8	48	160	200	288
— OR —					
Quick: number of strips	1	3	10	13	18
Template 6d	8	48	160	200	288
— OR —					
Quick: number of strips	1	3	9	12	16
Template 3f	32	80	128	160	192
— OR —					
Quick: number of strips	2	5	8	10	12
Light:					
Template 4l	4	24	80	100	144
— OR —					
Quick: number of strips	1	1	2	3	3
Template 1m	4	24	80	100	144
— OR —					
Quick: number of strips	1	2	4	5	7
Template 3a	312	508	852	936	1104
— OR —					
Quick: number of strips *	7	11	18	20	23

Template 4f	4	24	80	100	144
– OR –					
Quick: number of strips	1	1	3	4	5
Template 1h	4	24	80	100	144
– OR –					
Quick: number of strips	1	3	10	13	18
Template 4h	4	24	80	100	144
– OR –					
Quick: number of strips	1	1	4	5	8
Template 4a	16	40	64	80	96
– OR –					
Quick: number of strips	1	1	1	2	2
Template 1b	16	40	64	80	96
– OR –					
Quick: number of strips	1	2	3	4	4
Template 1a	16	16	16	16	16
– OR –					
Quick: number of strips	1	1	1	1	1
Borders:					
Number of 4⅞″ × 16½″ strips	4	—	—	—	—
Number of 4⅞″ × 14⅛″ strips	—	8	8	8	8
Number of 4⅞″ × 12¼″ strips	—	2	8	12	16
Backing: number of lengths	1	2	2	3	3

*Or use grid method for half-square triangles.

Quick cutting: Cut all of your quilt top fabrics crossgrain.
 • For 3j: Cut 1½″-wide strips. Then use template to mark and cut angles.
 • For 4l: Cut 3¼″-wide strips. Then cut to 3¼″ squares. Cut each square into *quarters diagonally.*
 • For 1m: Cut 2″-wide strips. Then cut to 2″ squares.
 • For 3a: Cut 1¾″-wide strips. Then cut to 1¾″ squares. Cut each square in *half diagonally.*
 • For 3h: Cut 1⅜″-wide strips. Then use template to mark and cut angles.
 • For 6d: Cut 4⅜″-wide strips. Then cut to 4⅜″ squares. Cut each square in *half diagonally.* Then use template to mark and cut angles.
 • For 4f: Cut 2⅜″-wide strips. Then cut to 2⅜″ squares. Cut each square in *half diagonally.*
 • For 1h: Cut 5¼″-wide strips. Then cut to 5¼″ squares.
 • For 4h: Cut 7⅞″-wide strips. Then cut to 7⅞″ squares. Cut each square into *quarters diagonally.*
 • For 3f: Cut 1⅜″-wide strips. Then use template to mark and cut angles.
 • For 4a: Cut 3″-wide strips. Then cut to 3″ squares. Cut each square into *quarters diagonally.*
 • For 1b: Cut 1⅞″-wide strips. Then cut to 1⅞″ squares.
 • For 1a: Cut 1⅜″-wide strips. Then cut to 1⅜″ squares.

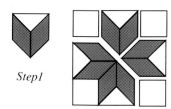

Step1

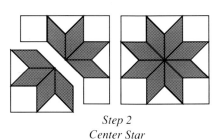

Step 2
Center Star

CONSTRUCTION

Center star: Use Y-seam construction.
1. Make four units, exactly as shown in the diagram.
2. Sew order (see diagrams). Press final seam open.

Sawtooth units:
1. For each block, make 56 half-square triangle units from Template 3a pieces.
2. Make four pieced strips, *each,* exactly as shown in the diagrams.
3. Make four corner units, exactly as shown in the diagram.
4. Make four pieced strips, *each,* exactly as shown in the diagrams.
5. Make four star point units, exactly as shown in the diagrams.
6. Join the units together in rows, exactly as shown in the diagram.
7. Attach the side triangles, exactly as shown in the diagram.

Make 4   Make 4

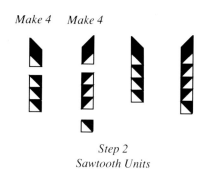

Step 2
Sawtooth Units

Make 4   Make 4

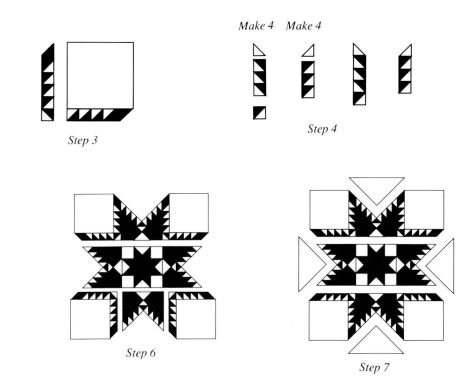

Step 3

Step 4

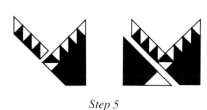

Step 5

Step 6

Step 7

BORDER

NOTE: The wall-size quilt has only eight-pointed stars in the corners, whereas all other sizes have stars evenly spaced around the borders, as shown in the photograph.

1. Make the required number of eight-pointed stars for the border and corner blocks. Use Templates 1b, 3f and 4a, following the instructions for center star given above.

2. Join the remaining light and dark Template 3a triangles to make half-square triangle units.

3. Make four corner units (see diagram).

4. Join the border strips to the eight-pointed stars, for all sizes except wall (see diagram).

5. Attach half-square triangle units to the border strips.

6. Sew the border strips and corner blocks to the quilt top.

Steps 3-5
Pieced Border

3a
1a
3f
4a
1b

CHAPTER 3

APPLIQUÉ QUILTS

A quiltmaker's first quilt is usually a pieced pattern like those found in Chapter Two. Often, the second, third, tenth and twentieth quilts are also pieced. Many accomplished quiltmakers never attempt an appliqué pattern. This may be because mastering a new sewing technique can seem like a daunting expedition into the unknown. But, remember: starting that first pieced quilt was a little scary, too.

We urge everyone interested in making quilts to create an appliqué. The woman or man is rare who does not appreciate a finely crafted bedcovering in a traditional appliqué pattern. And, for the more adventuresome, appliqué is a technique that allows for unlimited individuality and creativity; any idea, scene, story or motif can be rendered in appliqué. With its curves and natural shapes, appliqué can be adapted easily to your original design.

The history of appliqué is probably as old as sewing itself. Examples of early appliqué have been found in areas as far-flung as Siberia and Peru. Many of us regard the appliqué quilts of the nineteenth century as among our greatest treasures. They were made in a time when the development of power-driven machinery and the copper-plate gave quiltmakers an almost unlimited variety of cotton prints from which to choose.

At the same time, exquisite Broderie Perse appliqué quilts were also produced. A Broderie Perse quilt, printed chintz designs cut out and applied to a background fabric, is simple and less time-consuming to make than other appliqué quilts. And you can combine Broderie Perse with pieced, stenciled or other appliqué patterns. We have included Broderie Perse here so you can broaden your appliqué repertoire.

In past centuries the appliqué patterns chosen by quiltmakers were renditions of already established embroidery designs, like *Rose of Sharon* (see page 100). Thanks to our quiltmaking ancestors, today's traditional appliqué patterns have an even richer past upon which to draw.

Adaptability can be regarded as appliqué's greatest asset. Adapting an appliqué pattern is easy and fun. And it gives you enormous latitude in personalizing your quilt so there is no other exactly like it.

If there is a fabric, wallpaper, carpet, stained glass or architectural motif you'd like to use in your appliqué quilt, don't despair. In most of these cases, a copy machine with an enlarger will give you a black-and-white rendition of the design from which to craft your appliqué pattern.

Let your imagination run free: select a traditional pattern or create one of your own. Make an appliqué quilt.

HAND APPLIQUÉ: A PAPER-BASTING METHOD

SUPPLIES:

Background fabric: A stable 100% cotton, of even weave, or a good-quality sateen. Traditionally, white or off-white is used. Avoid a too tightly woven fabric as it is too difficult to appliqué and quilt through.

Fabric for individual shapes: A stable 100% cotton, of even weave.

Thread: A good quality thread that will not split or tangle: 100% cotton or 100% polyester rather than a blend works best for appliquéing the motifs. Look for the best match.

A thin, light-colored thread for basting

Tracing paper

Plain paper

Paper scissors

Fabric scissors

Embroidery scissors

Black ultra-fine permanent pen

#2.5 lead pencil

Drafting tape

#10 Between needle

3/4″ (size 12) sequin pins

Pressing surface

Light-colored towel

Steam iron

Fasturn® or metal strip and sewing machine (optional for making stems)

Plastic circle templates (optional)

Tweezers

Wide plastic ruler

In appliqué, designs are made by cutting pieces of one fabric and *applying* them to the surface of another. In Broderie Perse, you simply cut a shape or design from, say, a chintz and stitch it to a background fabric. But appliqué also allows you to create more intricate designs by combining several elements or shapes.

The paper-basted method of appliqué taught by Adele Ingraham, which we featured in *Quilts! Quilts!! Quilts!!!* and use here, allows you to make simple, elaborate or complex designs such as flowers, birds, animals, figures, hearts or symbols. You can make stylized or realistic designs because of the precision in making curves, points and V's. This method allows you to:

1. reproduce intricate shapes accurately from a line drawing;
2. duplicate shapes exactly;
3. place shapes flat on the background fabric;
4. handle very small shapes easily;
5. make smooth, even curves and sharp points and V's.

PREPARATION OF PATTERN

1. Using the ultra-fine permanent pen trace the entire design onto a piece of tracing paper. The larger appliqué patterns are presented in sections in the back of the book. For these patterns you must trace the sections from separate pages, aligning the sections to get the full pattern.

2. Trace the required number of shapes for the overall design onto a piece of plain paper (5 circles or 12 leaves, for example). Leave spaces between the shapes for easier cutting. Do not trace any stems: they will be made from bias strips of fabric. ✷ *Helpful hint:* Use a plastic circle template to make accurate circles. Mark the grainline on each shape.

3. Use your paper scissors to cut out all of the individual shapes. Since the shape you cut will be the shape you get, take time to cut accurately.

PREPARATION AND MARKING OF BACKGROUND FABRIC

1. Press your background fabric.

2. Cut out the background fabric, keeping the grainline straight, allowing a 1/4″ seam allowance on all sides.

3. Turn the background fabric to the wrong side and, with a lead pencil, write the word "Top" and indicate the direction of the lengthwise grain in the seam allowance at the top of the block.

4. With the right side of the background fabric facing up, center it on top of the overall traced or photocopied design. Hold it in place with drafting tape. Using a #2.5 lead pencil, lightly trace 1/16″ inside each shape. In addition, stems are marked with a single line through the middle. ✻ *Helpful hint:* When tracing a design onto fabric, tape the pattern to a daylight window and tape the piece of fabric over it. Then use a lead pencil to trace lightly inside the design.

PREPARATION OF STEMS

Three methods of making bias strips of fabric appropriate for stems are given below.

Method One

Since QUILTS! QUILTS!! QUILTS!!! was published, we have discovered a new tool for making stems which we feel to be quick and easy, with beautiful finished results.

The tool necessary for making strips of bias fabric used for stems is called a Fasturn®. It is a narrow brass tube which works with strips of fabric which are cut either on straight grain or on the bias. However, we recommend cutting the fabric strips on the bias, as often in appliqué you will want stems to meander or curve around a design. The tubes can be purchased in separate sizes or as a set of six graduated sizes. We like either tube #2, which makes 1/4″-wide finished stems, or tube #3, which makes 3/8″-wide finished stems. Complete instructions and illustrations accompany the Fasturn® tubes, which can be purchased at your quilt shop.

1. Follow the instructions that come with your Fasturn® tubes to construct your bias tubes.

2. After your bias tubes have been made, center the bias strip directly over the stem placement lines on the pattern, following the curves of the pattern. Cut the strip where appropriate, allowing a 1/4″ extension for overlapping shapes. Pin the bias strips into place on the pattern.

3. Press all bias strips while they are still pinned to the pattern. This will pre-shape the strips and prevent them from puckering.

4. Remove the strips from the pattern. They are now ready to be appliquéd to your background fabric.

Method Two

1. Cut a bias strip of fabric 1/2″ wide by 25″ long. This can be made from 1/2 yard of fabric.

2. Fold both 25″ edges 1/8″ to the wrong side and hold them in place with a small basting stitch. Press.

3. Complete Steps 2–4 in Method One above.

Method Three — Utilizing bias bars or 1/4″ flat metal strips

1. Cut a bias strip of fabric 7/8″ wide by 25″ long. This can be made from 1/2 yard of fabric.

2. Fold the bias strip in half lengthwise with the right side facing out.

3. Machine stitch along the lengths with an accurate 1/8″ seam allowance. This will create a tube.

4. Insert the metal strip into the fabric tube and place the seam line in the center of a flat side of the bar.

5. With the metal strip still inserted in the fabric, steam press on both sides of the fabric.

6. Remove the metal strip.

7. Complete Steps 2–4 in Method One above.

PINNING AND BASTING PAPER PATTERNS TO FABRIC

1. With the grainline marking facing you, lay the individual paper patterns on the wrong side of the fabric, leaving at least 1/2″ between shapes. The grainline marking on the paper pattern must correspond to the lengthwise grain of the fabric.

2. Pin the paper pattern in place with sequin pins.

3. Using small scissors, cut out the fabric around the shape, 1/4″ larger than the paper pattern.

4. Baste the paper pattern to the fabric. Remove the pins.

5. This step involves basting the seam allowance down to the wrong side of the paper pattern. Preparation for basting varies from shape to shape. Specific instructions follow:

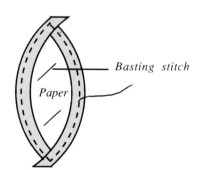

Basting stitch

Paper

   a. Leaves (and other shapes with points, such as hearts)

     (1) Thread your needle with a single strand of thread and place a knot in one end. With the paper pattern facing you, fold the seam allowance toward you.

     (2) Starting on one side of the shape (and not at its point), bring the needle up from the right side (so that the knot is on the right side). Take small running stitches to hold the seam allowance in place.

     (3) Stitch right up to the point, then fold the seam allowance from the opposite side of the shape and continue stitching. When you look at the right side of the shape, there may be an excess piece of fabric extending out beyond the point. This will be tucked under when the shape is sewn to the background fabric. *Do not cut it off.*

     (4) Continue around the shape. Cut the thread.

     (5) Press on the wrong, then right, side.

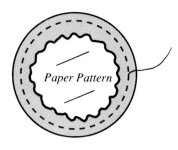

For hand appliqué work, use a single strand of thread and secure one end with a knot. With the right side of the motif facing up, bring the needle and thread from the underside up through the folded edge in the motif. Insert the tip of the needle directly behind and a little below the point where the thread emerges. Without pulling the thread through, slant the needle and bring it to the top side through the folded edge in the motif, approximately 1/16″ away from the previous stitch. Pull the thread through.

b. Circles
   (1) Thread your needle with a single strand of thread and place a knot in one end. With the paper pattern facing you, take small running stitches 1/8″ away from the edge of the paper pattern, drawing up the thread as you sew. This will distribute the fullness evenly. Continue all the way around the circle. This row of stitching will not be removed.
   (2) Baste again around the edge of the circle through all layers to hold the seam allowance flat.
   (3) Press on the wrong, then right, side.

c. Scallops (and shapes with V's, such as hearts)
   (1) At each V make a small, straight clip into the seam allowance, stopping 1/16″ from the edge of the paper pattern.
   (2) With the paper side up, fold the seam allowance towards you. Thread your needle with a single strand of thread and place a knot in one end. Bring the needle up from the right side (so that the knot is on the right side). Folding the clipped edges of the V out sideways to form an inverted V, take small running stitches to hold the seam allowance in place.
   (3) Continue around the shape. Cut the thread at the end.
   (4) Press on the wrong, then right, side.

PLACEMENT OF PAPER-BASTED PIECES TO A BACKGROUND FABRIC

1. Shapes which appear closest to the background fabric, or which will have other shapes extending over part of them, are positioned first. This generally applies to stems. Position the pre-shaped stems one at a time over the marked lines on the background fabric. Pin and then baste them in place.

2. Stitch them to the background fabric with a back whipstitch along both sides.

3. Leaves are placed on next. One at a time, pin, then baste, the leaves into position on the background fabric.

4. Starting on a curved side of the leaf, not at its point, stitch it in place using the back whipstitch. Stitch right up to the point. At the point, use the tip of your needle or your small scissors to tuck the excess fabric under the point. Take one extra, tiny stitch to hold it in place. Stitch around the opposite side, repeating the procedure at the other point and continuing around the curve, stopping 1/2″ from the starting point.

5. Remove the basting threads.

6. Use your tweezers to reach into the opening and remove the paper pattern.

7. Sew up the opening. End the stitching with two small backstitches on the wrong side.

8. Some small shapes are combined with larger shapes to form one unit before applying them to the background fabric, for example, centers to flowers or small flower buds to leaves. Place the smaller shape onto the larger shape, having their grainlines parallel. Hand stitch the small shape

in place using a back whipstitch, stopping in time to remove the paper pattern.

9. Flowers with or without centers are placed on next. Pin, and then baste, the flowers in place.

10. Stitch the flowers to the background fabric using a back whipstitch, stitching all the way around the shape. End with two small backstitches on the wrong side. Remove the basting threads.

11. Turn the design to the wrong side. Cut out the background fabric underneath the flower to within 1/4″ of the stitching line. This is done on any large shape to eliminate any excess bulk and prevent one color from shadowing through to another.

12. Finally, place the block, wrong side up, on a light-colored towel. Press firmly. Turn the block right side up and press lightly.

SUPPLIES:
Fabric: 10½″ square for background;
** 1/8 yard *each* of two shades of**
** pink; 1/4 yard of green**
Tracing paper
#2.5 lead pencil
Plain paper
Fabric scissors
Embroidery scissors
3/4″ (#12) sequin pins
#10 Between needle
Thread to match motif fabrics
Thin, light-colored thread for
** basting**
Pressing surface
Light-colored towel
Steam iron
Tweezers
Black ultra-fine permanent pen

PRACTICE EXERCISE: Making an 8″ appliqué block (corner of *Rose of Sharon*)
Use Templates 18b, 18c, 18d, 18e, and 18m.

1. Use the ultra-fine permanent pen to trace the entire design onto the tracing paper.

2. Lay the plain paper over the tracing paper and trace the following number of shapes for the overall design, remembering to mark the direction of the lengthwise grainline on each shape:

Template 18b — one	Template 18c — one
Template 18e — one	Template 18m — two
Template 18d — one	

3. Prepare the background fabric, lightly marking the placement of the shapes onto the right side. See "Preparation and Marking of Background Fabric."

4. Pin, then baste the paper patterns to the wrong side of the appropriate motif fabric. The grainline marking on the paper patterns must correspond to the lengthwise grain of the fabric. To prevent excess bulk, do not baste the bottom edge of shape 18b and shape 18c under, as shape 18b will be covered by shape 18c and shape 18c will be covered by shape 18d. Do not baste the inside edges of shapes 18m under, as they will be covered by shape 18e. See the instructions on pages 87–88 for working with points and V's.

5. Place shape 18b into position on the background fabric. Pin, baste and then use a back whipstitch to secure.

6. Place shape 18c into position on the background fabric. Pin, baste and then stitch in place.

7. Place shape 18m into position on the background fabric. Pin, baste and then stitch in place.

8. Place shapes 18e and then 18d into position on the background fabric. Pin, baste and then stitch in place.

9. Clip and remove all the basting threads. Carefully cut away the background fabric from behind the design, cutting to within 1/4″ of the outer-edge stitching lines.

10. Remove the paper patterns.

11. Press the completed design on its wrong, then right, side.

This completes the practice exercise for hand appliqué.

Corner of Rose of Sharon block

BRODERIE PERSE

SUPPLIES:

Background fabric: A stable 100% cotton of even weave, or a good-quality sateen. Traditionally, white or off-white is used. Avoid a too tightly woven fabric as it is too difficult to appliqué and quilt through.

Design fabric: Chintz with well-defined motifs (those motifs which are outlined in a darker color are preferable) or Broderie Perse fabric. Avoid using heavy decorator fabrics for the needle-turn method, although they are appropriate for the buttonhole method. Pre-wash (hand wash in warm water, no detergent) to pre-shrink, soften and make it easier to work with. □ *Warning:* Pre-washing may remove the glaze on some chintz fabrics. Experiment with a small sample before washing the entire piece.

Thread: A good quality thread that will not split or tangle: 100% cotton or 100% polyester rather than a blend works best for appliquéing the motifs. Look for the best match. If the motif has a thin outline of a different color, the thread should match the color of the outline; otherwise, match your thread with the motif. For the buttonhole method, use either a machine embroidery or a quilting thread. They will give very different results, so it is best to experiment. The machine embroidery thread tangles easily but will produce very fine stitches, whereas the quilting thread is easier to work with but the stitches look much heavier.

Thin, light-colored thread for basting

#10 Between needle

Fabric scissors

Small embroidery scissors

3/4″ (size 12) sequin pins

Pressing surface

Light-colored towel

Steam iron

Pinking shears (optional)

METHOD ONE: NEEDLE TURN

1. Cut your background fabric the desired finished size plus seam allowance. ✱ *Helpful hint:* Many fabrics will ravel badly while you are working with them. To preserve the edges, you can use pinking shears and cut a 1/2″ rather than the usual 1/4″ seam allowance. The excess can be trimmed off later. Some quiltmakers use tape to protect the edges; we do not advise using tape, as it leaves a sticky residue on the fabric which is difficult to quilt through. Remember to keep the lengthwise grainline consistent on all blocks. It is important in appliqué to use pieces of background fabric which are cut on straight grain. You can pull a thread if necessary to obtain a straight grain cut. To do so, make a small clip into the selvage of the fabric. Carefully grab a crosswise thread and gently pull. The fabric will gather along the thread line. Use your scissors to cut along the pulled thread line. If the thread should break before you reach the opposite selvage, cut on the thread line to where the gathers stop, reach in and grab the crosswise thread and continue pulling.

2. Cut out many motifs from your design fabric, cutting 1/8″ beyond the outer edges for turning under. Use 1/8″ rather than the usual 1/4″ allowance to eliminate bulk and to allow for easier turning with your needle. Often the motif is very small; the shape and detail would be difficult to achieve if the allowance were too wide. ✱ *Helpful hint:* Motifs with smooth edges are easier to turn under than those with jagged edges.

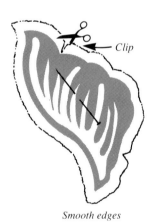  

Smooth edges   *Jagged edges*   *Jagged edges*

This does not mean that you must avoid using all motifs with jagged edges. Since you can create the shape of the finished edge with your needle, it is all right for you to even off a jagged edge to make stitching easier.

3. Place the cut motifs onto the background fabric in a pleasing arrangement. Some motifs may overlap others.

4. Pin, then hand baste the motifs into position. Do not allow the basting stitches to get closer than 1/4″ from the edges of the motifs, as you will need room for clipping the curves and V's and turning under a 1/8″ allowance.

Clip V

5. Press on the wrong, then right, side.

6. Use your small embroidery scissors to clip into the allowance around the curves, stopping a scant less than 1/16″ from the outline of the motif.

Outside curves: Cut a small triangle of allowance to eliminate excess bulk.

Inside curves: Make small clips into the allowance every 3/8″ to 1/2″ for ease in turning.

7. Thread your #10 Between needle with a single strand of thread (approximately 18″–20″ long) and secure one end with a knot.

8. Use the tip of your needle to turn the edges of the motifs under 1/8″, and hold them in place with the thumb of your free hand. The outline of the edge of the motif should rest along the folded edge. ✷ *Helpful hint:* The tip end of your embroidery scissors is helpful in turning under those areas which are difficult to turn with the needle.

9. Using a small back whipstitch, appliqué the motifs in place to the background fabric. It is not necessary to stitch those portions of the motifs which are overlapped by another motif. The underlying portion of the motifs should be cut away to avoid ridge lines occurring from excess bulk. ✷ *Helpful hint:* Work approximately 1/2″ to 1″ ahead of the stitches in turning the raw edges with the tip of your needle.

When working with points: Stitch right up to the tip of the point, then bring the needle and thread to the front side. With the tip of the needle, turn the allowance under along the opposite side of the point and continue sewing. If the point of the motif is too sharp and narrow it is all right to cheat a little and cut off the tip to create a wider point which will be easier to stitch. This will look just as effective.

When working with V's: At each V, make a small clip into the allowance, stopping just short of the outline of the motif. Stitch up to the crook of the V and bring the needle and thread to the front side. Use the tip of the needle to turn the allowance under along the other side of the V. Hold it in place with the thumb of your free hand. Take a stitch *very* close to the previous one to prevent the allowance from coming loose at the crook of the V. Continue stitching until your motif is completely sewn to the background fabric.

10. Remove the basting stitches.

11. Press on the wrong, then right, side.

METHOD TWO: BUTTONHOLE STITCH

Another method which has been traditionally used to attach the motifs to the background fabric is a small buttonhole stitch. This is also a good method to use because the stitches will form a cable along the raw edge of the motif, reinforcing the edges. Not only are the stitches decorative but they also give added strength to the motif. It is sometimes easier this way to achieve very small detail and sharp points and curves which you may not be able to achieve by turning under the allowance.

1. Cut your background fabric as described in Step 1 of Method One above.

2. Cut the motifs, leaving a 1/8″ allowance exactly as described in Step 2 of Method One above.

3. Place the motifs onto the background fabric in a pleasing arrangement. Some motifs may overlap others.

4. Pin, then hand baste them in place. Do not allow the basting stitches to get too close to the edges of the motif.

5. Press on the wrong, then right, side.

6. Thread your small #10 Between needle with a single strand of quilting or machine embroidery thread and secure one end with a knot. The color of the thread should match the background color of the motif fabric. Work very small buttonhole stitches along the edges of the motifs within the 1/8″ allowance. The stitches will be made *very* close together to prevent the cut edges of the allowance from raveling.

When stitching overlapped motifs, stitch up to within 1/2″ of the point where the two motifs overlap along their edges. Fold the overlying motif back over itself and with your embroidery scissors cut away the excess underlying motif, leaving a 1/4″ allowance beyond the edge of the overlying motif. Unfold the overlying motif and continue stitching. This step will prevent ridge lines caused from excess bulk.

7. Press on the wrong, then right, side.

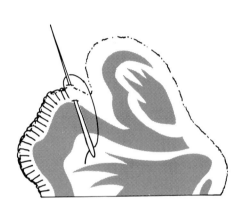

BUTTONHOLE STITCH:
See page 106 for instructions.

PRACTICE EXERCISE: We suggest that you take time to practice the techniques described above. You will be pleasantly surprised to find that the result is quite lovely and not nearly as difficult as it looks. Purchase a small amount of chintz or Broderie Perse fabric with well-defined motifs. Try to find ones with a variety of edges—curves, points and V's. Cut out a few motifs and arrange them onto a piece of background fabric. Pin and then baste them in place. Practice with both the needle-turn and buttonhole-stitch methods. For the buttonhole method, try using both quilting thread and machine embroidery thread. When you feel comfortable with one of the techniques, try your hand at applying it to one of the patterns such as the *Flower Garden Basket* shown on page 55, or create one of your own.

MACHINE APPLIQUÉ

SUPPLIES:

Thread: A good quality 100% cotton. Do not use machine embroidery thread, as it is too thin. ☐ *Warning:* **It is important to use the same thread both on the top and in the bobbin.**

Needle: #9 or #10 universal (not ballpoint)

Scissors: fabric, small embroidery and paper scissors

Ultra-fine permanent pen

Plain paper

Pellon Wonder-Under™ Transfer Web: turns your motif fabric into fusible fabric which will prevent the motif from pulling into the center and/or twisting.

Pellon Stitch-n-Tear®: a stabilizer which supports the background fabric

Sewing machine with zig zag setting

Machine appliqué foot which is open on the bottom, allowing the stitches to feed evenly

Pressing surface

Light-colored towel

Iron

Because appliqué with a machine can be inventive and saves lots of time, we urge you to try it. With experience and experimentation, you can develop your machine appliqué skills. Be patient: it takes time.

If you attempt machine work, you need to take time to get to know, care about and care for your machine.

• Ideally, you own a good machine with a zig zag stitch that makes a flat, smooth, even stitch. Skipped stitches, puckers and creeping have given machine appliqué a bad reputation. Practice making stitches with your machine.

• Treat your machine like a friend and learn everything possible about what it can and cannot do. Using a doodle cloth, practice the zig zag satin stitch around curves and corners.

• Learn to maintain your machine with proper needle and cleanings to keep it in good working order.

If you master the technical aspects of your machine, you will find machine appliqué a valuable addition to your quiltmaking repertoire. It is especially useful for a quilt which will receive heavy use and frequent washings, such as a child's quilt.

CHECK YOUR MACHINE BEFORE BEGINNING

For best results, your machine should be in good working order. Insert a new needle and remove any lint which has collected under the throat plate. Thread your machine. Set your machine on a medium-width zig zag and a very short stitch length. On a scrap of medium-weight fabric, check for the following:

• stitch width (approximately 1/8″ to 3/16″): wider stitches are suitable for quilts which require frequent washing, e.g., baby quilts;

• density of stitches: the stitches should be very close together but not stacked;

• even feeding.

• Does the bobbin thread pull to the front side? If so, slightly tighten the bobbin tension.

METHOD ONE: USING A PAPER PATTERN

1. Using the ultra-fine permanent pen trace the entire design onto a piece of paper. The larger appliqué patterns are presented in sections in the back of the book. For these patterns you must trace the sections from separate pages, aligning the sections to get the full pattern.

2. With the fusible (rough) side facing up, lay a piece of Wonder-Under™ over this paper pattern of your block. Use an ultra-fine permanent pen to trace around the desired shape. ✷ *Helpful hint:* If several shapes are required, use a large enough piece of Wonder-Under™ to trace several shapes at once, leaving at least 1/2″ between shapes. Keep those shapes which will be cut from the same fabric close together for ease in cutting later.

Original pattern

Wonder-Under (rough side)

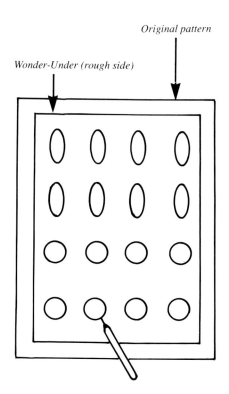

3. Use your paper scissors to cut the shapes (or groups of small shapes) apart, cutting outside the marked lines.

4. With the wrong side facing up, lay the motif fabric on your pressing surface. Place the marked side of the Wonder-Under™ on top of the motif fabric. ▣ Warning: Do not cut the piece of Wonder-Under™ larger than the motif fabric, as it will bond to your pressing surface when pressed.

5. Use a dry iron on medium setting to press the two layers together and bond the Wonder-Under™ to the motif fabric.

6. Use your fabric scissors to cut accurately *just inside* each marked shape.

7. Carefully peel away the thin paper layer from the smooth side of the Wonder-Under™.

8. With the right side facing up, lay your background fabric on your pressing surface. Position the shapes onto the background fabric in the desired arrangement. ✷ *Helpful hint:* Use a pencil to trace lightly the position of the shapes onto the background fabric.

9. Use a dry iron on medium setting to press *lightly* and bond the shapes to the background fabric. ▣ *Warning:* Avoid applying too much pressure, or you will not be able to adjust the shapes if necessary.

10. Cut a piece of Stitch-n-Tear® larger than the overall size of your block.

11. With the right side of the block facing up, center the block over the Stitch-n-Tear®. Lay this unit onto the bed of the sewing machine.

12. Thread your machine and bobbin with a color to match the shape to be stitched. It is best to change the thread with each new color.

13. Adjust the position of the design so that the edge of a shape is directly underneath the needle. Lower the presser foot and use the handwheel to insert the needle. The needle, positioned *on the right,* must enter the background fabric just to the right of the edge of the shape.

14. Continue turning the handwheel to complete the stitch. At this point you can adjust the width if necessary. Take note of this width position, as you will change it in the next step.

15. To lock the stitches and prevent the thread ends from coming loose, set the stitch width at 0 and take 3 stitches in place.

16. Return the stitch width to the setting determined in Step 14.

17. Continue stitching around the shape in a clockwise direction.

✷ *Helpful hints:*

Inside curve: Stop with the needle in the down position on the left-hand side. Raise the presser foot and pivot the fabric, lower the presser foot and continue stitching. Repeat as often as necessary to get around the curve.

Outside curve: Stop with the needle in the down position on the right-hand side. Raise the presser foot and pivot the fabric, lower the presser foot and continue stitching. Repeat as often as necessary to get around the curve.

Inside corner: Stitch up to the edge of the shape in the corner. With the needle in the down position on the left-hand side, raise the presser foot, pivot the fabric, lower the presser foot and continue stitching.

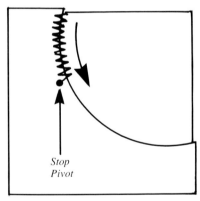

Inside curve

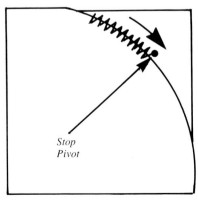

Outside curve

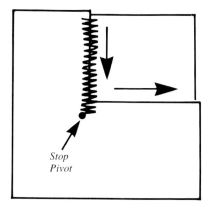

Inside corner

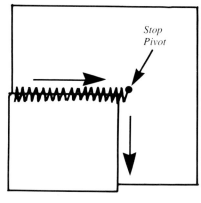

Outside corner

Outside corner: Stitch up to the edge of the shape in the corner. With the needle in the down position on the right-hand side, raise the presser foot, pivot the fabric, lower the presser foot and continue stitching.

Points and V's: Stitch to within 3/8" of the point or V and, without stopping the machine, gradually narrow the stitch width as you sew up to the end of the point or V. With the needle in the down position on the right-hand side for points and left-hand side for V's, raise the presser foot, pivot the fabric, lower the presser foot and continue stitching as you gradually increase the stitch width to its normal size.

18. Turn the fabric to the wrong side and gently remove all of the Stitch-n-Tear® stabilizer.

19. If the shape is large enough to require quilting stitches, *carefully* cut and pull away the background fabric and fusible web from the back of the shape, cutting up to the zig zag stitching lines. ✷ *Helpful hint:* Use your thumb to rub against and loosen the background fabric behind the motif. Use the tip of your small scissors to cut only into the background fabric.

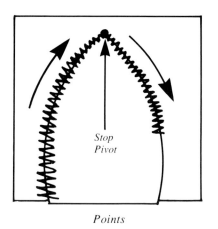

Points

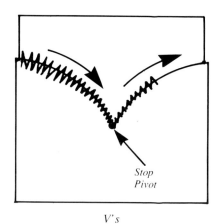

V's

METHOD TWO: USING BRODERIE PERSE MOTIFS

1. Cut out the desired motifs from your design fabric, leaving at least 1/2" around the outside edge of the shapes.

2. Fuse the printed motif to the Wonder-Under™ as described in Steps 4 and 5 in Method One.

3. Carefully cut out the printed motif, leaving approximately 1/8"–3/16" allowance around the outside edge. Carefully peel away the thin paper layer from the smooth side of the Wonder-Under™.

4. Position the motif on the background fabric and fuse in place as described in Step 9 in Method One.

5. Cut a piece of Stitch-n-Tear® and position the layers in your machine as described in in Steps 10 and 11 in Method One.

6. Thread your machine and bobbin with a color to match the background fabric.

7. Adjust the sewing machine and stitch around the motif as described in Steps 13 through 19 in Method One.

Fabric: 10″ square for background;
   1/8 yard *each* of three fabrics for
   motif
12″ square Pellon Wonder-Under™
10″ square Pellon Stitch-n-Tear®
Thread: 100% cotton in colors to
   match motif fabrics
Ultra-fine permanent pen
Tracing paper
Fabric scissors
Paper scissors
Small embroidery scissors
Sewing machine with appliqué foot
Pressing surface
Light-colored towel
Iron
Sharp lead pencil

Portion of Wedding Rose block

PRACTICE EXERCISE: Making a 9½″ block (portion of *Wedding Rose* block)
   Use Templates 14a, 14b, 14e, 14f and 14g.

1. Using the ultra-fine permanent pen, trace the entire design onto the tracing paper.

2. Using the ultra-fine permanent pen, trace the individual shapes onto the Wonder-Under™:

   main stem: make bias strip
   side stem: make bias strips
   leaf (Template 14g) — trace four
   flower (Template 14b) — trace two
   flower center (Template 14a) — trace two
   flower bud (Template 14e) — trace one
   flower calyx (Template 14f) — trace one

3. Use a dry iron on medium setting to fuse the Wonder-Under™ shapes to the appropriate motif fabrics.

4. Cut each fabric shape and peel away the smooth side of the Wonder-Under™.

5. Finger press diagonal folds into the background fabric for ease in positioning the shapes, or you can lay the background fabric over the traced pattern and use a pencil to trace *lightly* the position of the shapes.

6. With its right side facing up, lay the background fabric on a flat pressing surface. Then position the shapes onto the background fabric in the following order: side stems, center stem, leaves, flowers, flower centers, flower bud, flower calyx.

7. *Lightly* touch the shapes with the iron to bond them to the background fabric.

8. Thread your machine with a color to match the stems and leaves. Set the width and length on your machine to make a small, even satin stitch.

9. Try the stitch on a doodle cloth. Then, when you are satisfied, lay the block onto the bed of the sewing machine.

10. Stitch the motifs in the following order, with Stitch-n-Tear®, changing the color of thread as necessary:

   side stems
   center stem
   leaves
   flower centers
   flowers
   flower bud
   flower calyx

11. Press the block on its wrong side. Then remove the Stitch-n-Tear®.

12. Remove the background fabric from behind the flowers, flower bud and flower calyx.

This completes your practice exercise for machine appliqué.

WEDDING ROSE

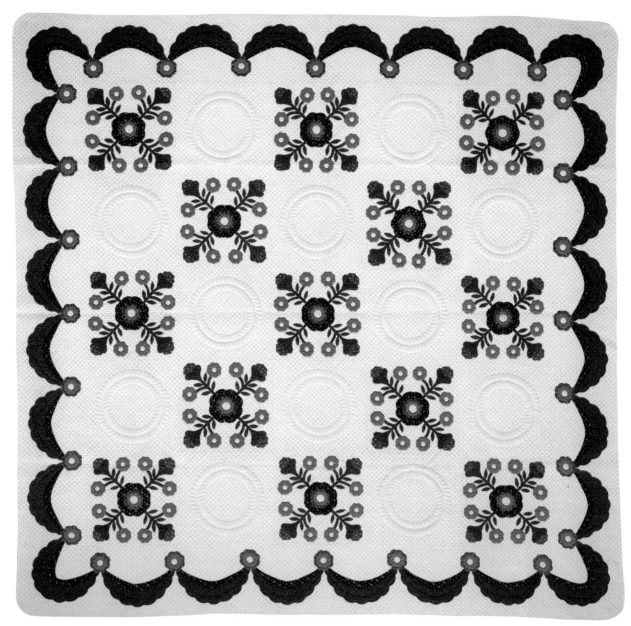

Designed by Adele Ingraham and made by friends for Laura Nownes

Block size: 15″

Techniques: Appliqué (Templates 14a, 14b, 14c, 14d, 14e, 14f, 14g, 15b, 15c, 16b, 16c and 18a) and trapunto

Setting: Straight

Fabric suggestions: Light background and five fabrics for appliquéd blocks and borders.

	Wall	Twin	King
Finished size	69″ × 69″	69″ × 99″	99″ × 99″
Blocks set	3 × 3	3 × 5	5 × 5
# appliqué blocks	5	8	13
# trapunto blocks	4	7	12
# side swag units	12	16	20
# corner swag units	4	4	4

YARDAGE

	Wall	Twin	King
Background and binding (bias)	5½	7	10
Navy	⅝	1	1¼
Rust	½	⅝	¾
Light Blue	⅜	¾	1
Yellow	⅛	¼	⅜
Green	1¾	2¼	3
Backing	4¼	6	8¾
Inner lining for trapunto blocks	1	2	2¾

CUTTING

	Wall	Twin	King
Background:			
Two border strips at 12½″ ×	73″	73″	103″
Two border strips at 12½″ ×	73″	103″	103″
Number of 16″ squares	9	15	25
Navy:			
Template 14d	5	8	13
Template 16b	12	16	20
Template 15b	4	4	4
Rust:			
Template 14c	5	8	13
Template 14e	20	32	52
Template 18a	16	20	24
Light Blue:			
Template 14b	61	92	141
Yellow:			
Template 14a	61	92	141
Green:			
Template 14f	20	32	52
Template 16c	12	16	20
Template 14g	80	128	208
Template 15c	4	4	4
¼″ finished bias strips: number of yards	5	8	13

Inner lining: number of 16″ squares	4	7	12
Backing: number of lengths	2	2	3

CONSTRUCTION

Instructions are given for hand appliqué, although machine techniques could be used if desired.

1. Prepare the pattern and paper baste the individual shapes. It is not necessary to turn under and baste the bottom edge of shape 14e, as it will be covered by shape 14f. The same applies to the top edge of shape 16c, as it will be covered by shape 16b.

2. Lightly mark the placement of the shapes onto the background fabric.

3. Make the center flower units for the blocks, using shapes 14a, 14b, 14c and 14d. Remember to cut away the fabric from the back of the shapes to eliminate bulk.

4. Make the small flower units for the blocks, using shapes 14a and 14b.

5. Make the flower units for the borders, using shapes 14a, 14b and 18a.

6. Make the bud units for the blocks, using shapes 14e and 14f.

7. Prepare the bias stems using one of the methods described in the general instructions.

8. Position the stems onto the background fabric blocks. Pin, hand baste and then appliqué in place.

9. Pin, hand baste and then appliqué the remaining shapes to the background fabric block in the following order:

    Center flower unit (Templates 14a, 14b, 14c and 14d)
    Small flower units (Templates 14a and 14b)
    Bud unit (Templates 14e and 14f)
    Leaves (Template 14g)

10. Prepare the required number of trapunto alternate blocks. Purchase a plastic template or create your own design which will fit into a 15″ square. Refer to Chapter Five for help with trapunto.

11. Trim all blocks to 15½″.

12. Set the blocks together, alternating the appliqué and trapunto.

13. Attach the border strips, mitering the corners and trimming any excess length.

14. Paper baste the required number of side swag and corner swag units. For side swags use Templates 16b and 16c, and for the corner swags use Templates 15b and 15c. It is not necessary to turn under and baste the top edges of shapes 15c and 16c, as they will be covered with other shapes.

15. Position all of the swag and flower units onto the border strips. NOTE: The block size was reduced slightly to fit into this book. As a result, the placement of the border swag will differ from the photo. A flower unit will be positioned at the seam joining each block and a swag unit will fit in between each flower unit.

16. Pin, hand baste and then appliqué all shapes to the border strips. Remember to remove the paper patterns from all shapes.

ROSE OF SHARON

Made by Hattie Bornett Ramsay, 1928; collection of Diana McClun

Block size: 15″

Techniques: Appliqué (Templates 16d, 17a, 17b, 17c, 17d, 17e, 17f, 17g, 18b, 18c, 18d, 18e, 18f, 18g, 18h, 18j, 18k and 18m)

Setting: Straight

Fabric suggestions: Muslin color for background, light pink, medium pink, dark pink, medium green and dark green.

	Crib/Wall	Twin	Double	Queen	King
Finished size	52″×52″	67″×82″	82″×82″	82″×97″	112″×97″
Blocks set	2×2	3×4	4×4	4×5	6×5
# inside blocks	—	2	4	6	12
# side blocks	—	6	8	10	14
# corner blocks	4	4	4	4	4

YARDAGE

	Crib/Wall	Twin	Double	Queen	King
Muslin	3¼	5	6⅜	7¼	10
Light pink	¾	1¼	1¾	2	2⅜
Medium pink	1	1¾	2	2¼	2¾
Dark pink	⅜	½	½	⅝	¾
Medium green	¾	1¾	2	2¼	2½
Dark green	½	⅝	⅝	¾	1
Backing & bias binding	4	5¾	6	6¾	9¾

CUTTING

	Crib/Wall	Twin	Double	Queen	King
Muslin:					
Borders:					
Two at 11½" ×	56"	73"	88"	88"	104"
Two at 11½" ×	56"	87"	88"	104"	120"
Blocks: number of 16" squares	4	12	16	20	30
Light pink:					
Template 17d	4	12	16	20	30
Template 18j	8	14	16	18	22
Medium pink:					
Template 17c	4	12	16	20	30
Template 17a	4	12	16	20	30
Template 18c	8	14	16	18	22
Template 18f	8	14	16	18	22
Template 18k	8	14	16	18	22
Dark pink:					
Template 17b	4	12	16	20	30
Template 18b	8	14	16	18	22
Template 18m	8	8	8	8	8
Medium green:					
Template 17e	32	96	128	160	240
Template 17f	32	96	128	160	240
Template 17g	32	96	128	160	240
Template 18d	4	10	12	14	18
Template 18e	4	4	4	4	4
Template 18h	8	14	16	18	22
Template 18g	8	14	16	18	22
Stems: # yards ¼"-wide finished	2	6	8	10	15
Dark green:					
Vines: # yards ⅝"-wide finished	1½	6	8	11	16½
– OR –					
Template 16d	8	34	48	62	98

CONSTRUCTION

Instructions are given for hand appliqué, although machine techniques could be used.

1. Prepare the pattern and paper baste the individual shapes. It is not necessary to turn under and baste the bottom edges of shapes 18b, 18c, 18f and 18m and the top edges of shapes 18h and 18j, as they will each be covered by other shapes.

2. Lightly mark the placement of the shapes onto the background fabric. Note the following:

    Inside blocks have four vines and no flower bud units;

    Side blocks have three vines and one flower bud unit;

    Corner blocks have two vines and two flower bud units.

3. Make the center flower units for each block, using shapes 17a, 17b, 17c and 17d. Remember to cut away the fabric from the back of the shapes to eliminate bulk.

4. Prepare the flower bud units, using shapes 18f and 18g.

5. Prepare the border flower units, using shapes 18b, 18c and 18d.

6. Prepare the corner flower units, using shapes 18b, 18c, 18d, 18e and 18m.

7. Prepare the swag units, using shapes 18h, 18j and 18k.

8. Prepare the ¼″ bias stems, using one of the methods described earlier in this chapter.

9. Prepare the vines, using either the Fasturn® tool or Template 16d.

10. Position the stems and vines onto the background fabric blocks. Pin, hand baste and then appliqué them in place.

11. Pin, hand baste and then appliqué the remaining shapes to the appropriate background fabric blocks in the following order:

    Flower bud units;

    Center flower units;

    Leaves.

12. Trim all blocks to 15½″.

13. Set the blocks together. Double-check the placement of vines and bud units with the photograph before sewing.

14. Attach the border strips, mitering the corners and trimming any excess length.

15. Position the swag and flower units onto the border strips. A flower unit is positioned directly opposite the seam joining the blocks.

16. Pin, hand baste and then appliqué the swags and flower units to the border strips. Remember to remove the paper patterns from all shapes.

17. Use your C-Thru ruler to measure from the edge of the swag out to mark a line for the scalloped edge of the quilt top.

OLD ENGLISH FLOWER GARDEN

Arlene Lane

An original design by Arlene Lane

Techniques: Broderie Perse appliqué and trapunto
Fabric suggestions: Chintz design fabric for cut-out motifs; light-colored cotton
   background.

If you wish to copy the center and feather trapunto designs precisely, full-size
patterns can be purchased directly from Adele Ingraham, 204 Dundee Way,
Benicia, CA 94510.

	Crib/Wall
Finished size	43½″ × 51″

YARDAGE

	Crib/Wall
Front fabric (includes binding)	2
Design fabric	The design of the fabric will determine the yardage.
Backing	1½

CONSTRUCTION

1. Create or choose trapunto patterns and make a paper pattern for each of them.

2. Select a group of floral cut-outs to make a circular floral wreath and the corner areas. Pin, then baste them into place on the background fabric.

3. Transfer your trapunto patterns to the background fabric. See "Tracing the Design Onto Fabric," Chapter Five.

4. Use one of the appliqué techniques to sew the cut-outs to your background fabric.

5. Outline the trapunto designs with quilting stitches. See "Outlining the Designs," Chapter Five.

6. Fill the outlined trapunto designs with yarn. See "Filling Channels" and "Filling Other Shapes," Chapter Five.

7. Block the quilt top. See Step 7 of "Trapunto for Whole-Cloth Quilts," Chapter Five.

8. Mark your background quilting designs. (Diagonal lines are started from the corners and angled to the center. Stop at the edge of the central motif. Reverse directions at each corner; this helps to keep the quilt from buckling when ¼″ spacing is used.)

9. Baste the quilt top, batting and backing fabric together.

10. Quilt around all the cut-out motifs and trapunto. Quilt the background filling. Use stipple quilting in appropriate areas. See "Stipple Quilting" in Chapter Six.

11. Bind your quilt with a fine corded binding.

CHAPTER 4

CRAZY QUILTS

 By the middle of the nineteenth century, an ornamental Crazy quilt was being made by women throughout America and the United Kingdom. It was decorated with laces and ribbons, beads and paint, feathers and yarn. Its primary fabrics were silks, satins, taffetas and velvets. And it was embellished with a wide variety of embroidery stitches and motifs.

In the Victorian period, from approximately 1870 to 1900, most quiltmakers made at least one Crazy quilt. And women who chose not to be quiltmakers did crazy patchwork as well. Women's magazines were filled with advertisements and articles about the Crazy quilt. Fabric and sewing-machine companies offered patterns. Through mail-order companies, women could receive pre-cut fabrics to start their Crazy projects, and there were even companies which sold completed embroidered and painted motifs (and entire Crazy quilt blocks) that a woman could purchase and include in her creation.

In short, Crazy quilts were a craze, and they epitomize to many the excesses (as we now regard them) of the Victorian decorative era.

A Crazy quilt is composed of blocks constructed from a variety of irregular shapes in a wide range of colors and textures sewn in a random arrangement to a foundation fabric. Embroidery, paint and a wide selection of three-dimensional objects (like beads) may decorate the surface. Lace, ruffles or other trimmings may decorate the edge of the finished quilt.

In recent years, over-the-counter trimmings have greatly improved. As a result, there is a wide selection of braids, laces and ribbons available to the quiltmaker. Add to these the almost infinite variety of beads and small decorative objects one can buy, and the materials available to decorate your Crazy quilt are unlimited.

We strongly recommend that beginners and experienced quiltmakers try their hand at a Crazy quilt. The medium is not demanding and it gives you total freedom to create something you will love. When you select bits and pieces of collected fabrics and collage them, mixing a variety of shapes and textures, you become totally free: no more patterns to follow, no more precision piecing. It is this freedom that makes crazy patchwork so exciting—and spontaneous. You can be as elaborate and excessive or as simple and orderly as your taste demands of you.

We also recommend this style of quilt to embroiderers and needle-workers. Here is a quilt you can make that employs your very important talents and showcases them to their best advantage. If you take a minute to look at the antique Crazy quilt on page 114, you will see that it is brimming over with decorative embroidery stitches.

STITCHES AND EMBELLISHMENTS

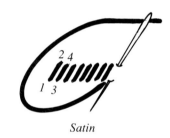

Satin

SATIN STITCH

Use a single strand of thread with a knot in one end. Bring the needle and thread from the back side up at 1. Insert the needle down at 2, up at 3, down at 4, etc. Keep the stitches close together and not too long, so they will lie flat and cover the background fabric.

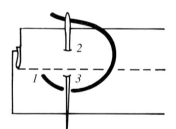

BLANKET/BUTTONHOLE

This stitch is worked from left to right. Use a single strand of thread in the needle with a knot in one end. Bring the needle from the back side up at 1. Next, insert the needle into the fabric at 2. Do not pull the thread through. Then, with the thread in back of the point of the needle, bring the point of the needle up again at 3. Pull the needle and thread through. Repeat, inserting at 4 and coming up again at 5, etc. A blanket stitch is simply a widely spaced buttonhole stitch.

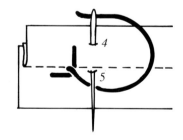

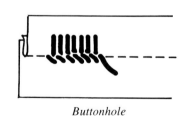

Buttonhole

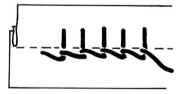

Blanket

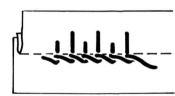

Blanket variation

CROSS

Since you will probably be making a series of cross stitches, you will want to make all of the half stitches in one direction, then complete the crosses in the other direction. Use a single strand of thread in the needle

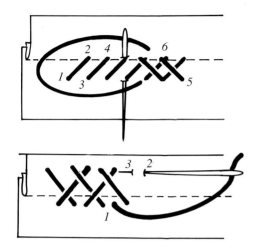

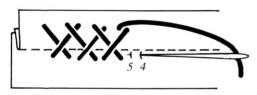

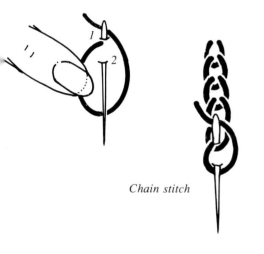

Herringbone

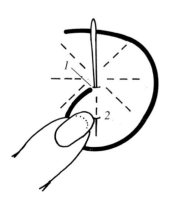

Chain stitch

with a knot in one end. Bring the needle and thread up from the back side at 1. Insert the needle down at 2 (just over the folded edge) and, without pulling the thread through, bring it up again at 3. Pull the needle and thread through. Insert the needle at 4 and continue all the way across. Return with movements 5 and 6 in the opposite direction to cross.

HERRINGBONE

This stitch is worked from left to right. Use a single strand of thread in the needle with a knot in one end. Bring the needle from the back side up at 1. With the thread above the folded line, insert the needle at 2, then come up at 3. Pull the needle and thread all the way through. With the thread below the folded edge and keeping the thread to the right-hand side, insert the needle at 4. Then come up at 5. Pull the needle and thread all the way through. Continue in this sequence. Point 5 will become 1 for the next sequence.

CHAIN

This stitch is worked from top to bottom. Use a single strand of thread in the needle with a knot in one end. Bring the needle and thread from the back side up at 1. Insert the needle down again at 1. Do not pull the thread through. Hold the thread down with your free thumb, while bringing the needle up at 2, making sure that the thread lies under the point of the needle. Now pull the needle and thread through to form a stitch. Repeat (number 2 becomes the new number 1).

LAZY DAISY

This stitch is worked in a circle and gives the appearance of flower petals. Use a single strand of thread with a knot in one end. Bring the needle and thread from the back side up at 1 and insert it down again at 1 without pulling the thread through. Hold the thread off to the side with your free thumb while bringing the needle up at 2, making sure the thread lies under the needle. Now pull the needle and thread through. Hold the thread with your free hand while inserting the needle at 3, on the opposite side of the loop, to hold it secure. Bring the needle out again at 4 and repeat the sequence to make another petal. Continue in this sequence until all the desired petals have been worked.

Lazy Daisy

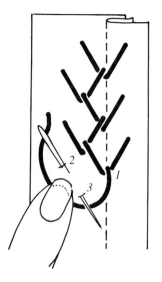
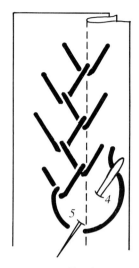

Feather

FEATHER

This stitch is worked from top to bottom. Use a single strand of thread in the needle with a knot in one end. Bring the needle up from the back side at 1. Insert the needle at 2 and, while holding the thread off to the side with your free thumb and keeping the thread under the tip of the needle, bring the needle up at 3. Pull the needle and thread all the way through. Insert the needle at 4 and, while holding the thread off to the side with your free thumb and keeping the thread under the tip of the needle, bring the needle up at 5. Pull the needle and thread all the way through. Continue this sequence. Point 5 will become 1 for the next sequence. Alternate this movement from left to right.

OPEN CRETAN

This stitch is worked from left to right. Use a single strand of thread in the needle with a knot in one end. Bring the needle up from the back side at 1. With the needle pointing toward you, insert it at 2, then bring it out at 3, which is directly below 2. Making sure that the thread lies under the needle, pull the needle and thread all the way through. With the needle pointing away from you, insert it at 4, then bring it out at 5, which is directly above 4. Making sure the thread lies under the needle, pull the needle and thread all the way through. Continue in this sequence, keeping points 3 and 5 close to the folded edge for maximum security.

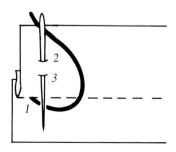
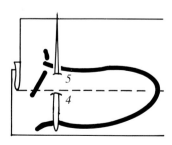
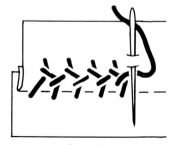

Open Cretan

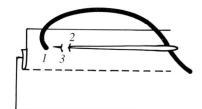

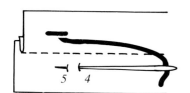

CHEVRON

This stitch is worked from left to right. Use a single strand of thread in the needle with a knot in one end. Bring the needle and thread from the back side up at 1. Next, with the thread above, insert the needle into the fabric at 2 and, without pulling the thread through, bring the needle up again at 3 (a point halfway between 1 and 2). Pull the needle and thread all the way through. Insert the needle at 4 and bring it up again at 5 and pull the needle and thread all the way through. (The distance between 4 and 5 is the same as between 1 and 3.) With the thread below, insert the needle at 6 and bring it up again at 4. With the thread below, insert the needle at 7 and bring it up at 8. Continue this sequence. Point 8 will become 1 for the next sequence.

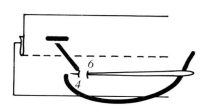

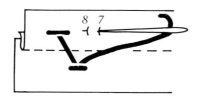

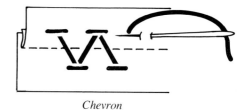

Chevron

ROSETTE

Use a single strand of thread with a knot in one end. Bring the needle and the thread from the back side up at 1. Insert the needle at 2 and, holding the thread off to one side with your free thumb, bring it out again at 1. Do not bring the needle completely through. Make several coils of thread beneath the needle. Holding the coils firmly so as not to lose the wraps, carefully pull the needle and thread through the wraps. Bring the needle across the coils and insert it through the fabric under the coils near point 2. Bring the needle and thread up from the back side at a point directly opposite the previous holding stitch. Insert the needle through the fabric under the coils near point 3. Take a backstitch and knot it.

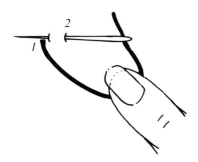

Rosette

FRENCH KNOT

Use a single strand of thread with a knot in one end. Pull the needle and thread all the way through to the front side. Hold the thread taut with your free hand and wrap it two or three times around the point of

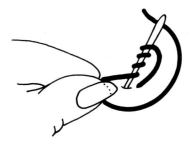

French knot

the needle. Keep the tension on the thread firm, so as not to lose the wraps. Insert the needle slightly to one side of the point at which it originally emerged. Pull the needle and thread through to the back side, holding the thread firm with the free hand so that a knot is formed on the top side. Take a backstitch and knot it.

BULLION KNOT

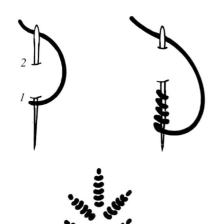

Bullion knot

Use a single strand of thread with a knot in one end. Bring the needle and the thread up from the back side at 1. Insert the needle at 2 and, without pulling the thread through, bring it out again at 1. Wrap the point of the needle 6 or 7 times with the thread. Holding the wraps with the thumb of your free hand, carefully pull the needle and thread through the wraps. Re-insert the needle at point 2 and pull the needle and thread through to the back side. To secure your knot, take a backstitch and knot it.

MAKING CRAZY BLOCKS

RECOMMENDED MATERIALS

Foundation Fabric
Loosely woven, lightweight loose flannel or any fabric which will allow the needle to go through easily

Fabrics for Patches
NOTE: It is *not* recommended to combine fabrics, as they are treated differently when washed. However, if you plan to dry clean your quilt, you can combine silks with cottons, for example.
Cotton—100% polished; cotton/polyester
Wool—lightweight 100%; wool/polyester
Silk—neckties work well (make sure they are clean); silk/polyester
Brocade
Damask
File

Moire
Velvet — lightweight velveteen

Threads and Trims
Threads — metallic, buttonhole, twist, embroidery (use 2–3 strands), rayon embroidery, perle cotton #8, linen, silk
Ribbons
Lace
Buttons
Beads
Yarn

CUTTING THE FABRICS

1. Cut a piece of foundation fabric at least 1″ larger than the desired finished size of the block. This excess is required to allow for any decrease in size which may be caused by all of the stitching. The block will be trimmed and squared up after all of the stitches have been applied.

2. Randomly cut shapes from the desired fabrics. Pieces do not have to be cut following the grainline, which means all scraps can be used. There is no waste. ✱ *Helpful hint:* Crazy patchwork is a wonderful way to use up all those odd-sized scraps you end up with after making a quilt and despair at throwing away.

Cut various shapes and sizes — straight lines as well as curves. When cutting the fabric shapes, keep in mind that a 3/8″ allowance will be turned under on all sides. A 3/8″ rather than the usual 1/4″ allowance is needed, since the edges of the shapes are simply turned under themselves and stitched in place. The additional 1/8″ gives more control and helps prevent the shapes from separating. Therefore, do not cut pieces *too* small.

TRADITIONAL (HAND) METHOD

The starting point for placement of the fabric shapes onto the foundation fabric can be in the center or anywhere else. The size of the block and its shape will often determine the starting point. For example, a 12″ square is a workable size, so you may choose to work from the center out. However, if you are working on a long, rectangular piece, it may be more convenient to work from one side to the opposite side. Although traditionally, it is believed, most Crazy blocks were begun near the center, whatever starting point feels more comfortable and appropriate is best.

1. Place a fabric shape which has at least four edges in the center of the foundation fabric. Use a few sequin pins to secure it in place. *Do not fold under the raw edges,* as they will be covered with overlying fabric shapes.

2. Place more fabric shapes around the first shape, turning under all of the raw edges which overlap the first shape. Be certain the overlying fabric shapes extend a full 3/8″ in from the raw edges of the first fabric shape. Secure the folded edges with sequin pins.

SUPPLIES:
Fabric scissors
Foundation fabric
Fabric shapes
Sequin pins, 3/4″ (#12) steel
Hand sewing needle
Needle, #5 Between
Threads and trims
Small embroidery scissors
Sewing machine
Thin, light-colored thread for basting (optional)
Wide plastic ruler

3. Continue in the same manner with additional fabric shapes, working out to the edges of the foundation fabric.

4. After the fabric shapes have been pinned in place, you can choose either to hand baste the shapes in place and remove the pins or to work with the block as is, leaving the pins in place. Basting is a helpful step, because the embroidery threads may tend to get caught in the pins as you stitch. ✱ *Helpful hint:* If you are working on a large block, you may want to pin, then baste one section at a time.

5. Now the fun begins! You are ready to start adding the embroidery stitches and embellishments. Use some from our list of stitches and embellishments, or any of your own choice. Be creative. In order to hold the fabric shapes securely, be sure that the stitches go all the way through to the back side of the foundation fabric. Always secure the folded edges of all fabric shapes with stitches.

6. Don't forget to embroider your name, the date and, possibly, a message on at least one of the blocks.

7. Trim the excess fabric and square up the blocks to measure your finished size plus 1/4″ seam allowance. Machine baste around the blocks 1/8″ from the edges.

8. The blocks are now ready to be included in your quilt.

QUICK (MACHINE) METHOD

In this method, fabric shapes are sewn onto the foundation fabric with a sewing machine.

1. Place a fabric shape right side up on the foundation fabric (starting either in the center or in a corner).

2. Lay another shape wrong side up on top of the first shape. Stitch the two shapes together along one edge with a 1/4″ seam, stitching through all thicknesses.

3. Fold the top shape back over the stitching line and finger press.

4. Lay another shape wrong side up, matching one of its sides to an unsewn side of the first shape. Stitch the two shapes together with a 1/4″ seam through all thicknesses.

5. Fold the shape back over the stitching line and finger press.

6. Continue working in the same manner until the entire block is sewn with fabric shapes.

7. Now it is time to add the embroidery stitches and embellishments. Use some from our suggested list or any of your own choice.

8. Trim the excess fabric and square up the blocks to measure your finished size plus 1/4″ seam allowance. Machine baste around the blocks 1/8″ from the edges.

9. The blocks are now ready to be included in your quilt.

SUPPLIES:
Fabric scissors
Foundation fabric
Fabric shapes
Sewing machine
Cotton or cotton/polyester thread
for sewing machine
Threads and trims
Needle, #5 Between
Small embroidery scissors
Large C-Thru ruler

CONSTRUCTING YOUR QUILT

After individual blocks are completed with stitches and embellishments, you are ready to sew them together. Additional stitches, embellishments and trims can be added after construction to hide the seams where the blocks are joined. You might decide to use the block as is and make it into a pillow or pincushion. In that case, you would finish off the edges in a manner appropriate to your particular project.

No batting layer is recommended, but if you are using a lightweight backing fabric and desire a little more stability, a lightweight flannel can be used.

Traditionally crazy quilts are tied, then bound, rather than being hand quilted, since quilting would interfere with the embroidery and embellishments.

TYING YOUR QUILT

SUPPLIES:
Cotton darning needle, #1
Perle cotton thread
Small embroidery scissors

This next step gives you knots on the right side of your quilt. If you prefer to hide the knots on the back side of the quilt, simply reverse the process.

1. Layer the backing and quilt top on a flat surface or in a frame.

2. Thread the cotton darning needle with a double thickness length of perle cotton (cut about a 60″ length of thread). Do not knot the end.

3. Choose a point in the center of the quilt where you would like to make a tie. Poke the needle down through all thicknesses and come up approximately 1/8″ away.

4. Move to the next spot to be tied and take a small stitch.

5. Working in one direction, continue across the quilt until you have run out of thread. You will want to take the stitches all in one direction.

6. Re-thread the needle and continue stitching until the entire quilt top is done.

7. With scissors, clip the threads between the stitches.

8. Tie a square knot at each point.

9. Trim off any excess thread if the tails are too long.

PRACTICE EXERCISE: No practice exercise is given for the techniques, but we strongly recommend that you take time to practice making the embroidery stitches.

Suggested Reading

McMorris, Penny. *Crazy Quilts*. New York: E. P. Dutton, Inc., 1984.

Montano, Judith. *The Crazy Quilt Handbook*. Lafayette, Calif.: C&T Publishing, 1986.

CRAZY QUILT

Maker unknown, c. 1880–1900; collection of Diana McClun

Block size: 9″
Techniques: Crazy patchwork, embroidery
Setting: Straight
Fabric Suggestions: Variety of scraps—cotton or silk and velvet.

	Crib/Wall	Twin	Double	Queen	King
Finished size	45″ × 54″	72″ × 90″	81″ × 90″	90″ × 90″	108″ × 99″
Blocks set	5 × 6	8 × 10	9 × 10	10 × 10	12 × 11
Total blocks	30	80	90	100	132

YARDAGE

	Crib/Wall	Twin	Double	Queen	King
Foundation fabric	2¼	5⅜	6	6⅝	9
Backing	3½	5½	5½	8	8¾

CONSTRUCTION

1. Make the required number of blocks, using one of the methods described in the general instructions.
2. Join the blocks together.
3. Add stitches to cover the seams joining the blocks.
4. This quilt has been tied, with the knots on the back side.
5. Additional backing fabric has been allowed to bring the edges of the backing to the front side, creating a binding. Hand stitch it in place.

FAN

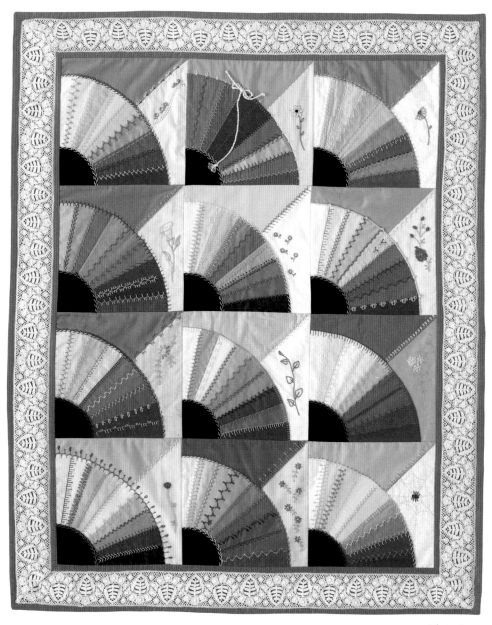

Claire Jarratt

Block size: 9″
Grid category: Circular
Techniques: Crazy patchwork with Templates 11a, 11b and 11c
Setting: Straight
Fabric suggestions: Variety of solid fabrics

	Crib/Wall	Twin	Double	Queen	King
Finished size	34″×43″	70″×88″	79″×88″	88″×97″	106″×97″
Blocks set	3×4	7×9	8×9	9×10	11×10
Total blocks	12	63	72	90	110

YARDAGE

	Crib/Wall	Twin	Double	Queen	King
Black	⅛	⅝	⅝	1	1⅛
Scraps to total	1¾	7	8	9¾	12
Border (mitered)	1⅜	2⅝	2⅝	3	3⅛
2½"-wide lace	5	9½	10	10¾	11¾
Backing	1⅜	5¼	5¼	8½	8½

CUTTING

	Crib/Wall	Twin	Double	Queen	King
Template 11c*	12 & 12R	63 & 63R	72 & 72R	90 & 90R	110 & 110R
Template 11b	108	567	648	810	990
Template 11a	12	63	72	90	110
Border: width	4"	4"	4"	4"	4"
Backing: number of lengths	1	2	2	3	3

*R = Reverse template on fabric.

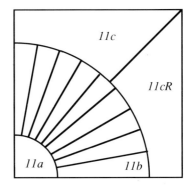

CONSTRUCTION

1. Sew nine Template 11b pieces together for each fan.
2. Sew a Template 11c to a Template 11cR for each block.
3. Turn the top edge of each fan under 1/2". Press lightly to hold the fold.
4. Pin and then baste each fan to each pair of background pieces, extending 1/4" onto the background.
5. Turn the curved edge of each Template 11a piece under 1/4".
6. Pin and then baste each Template 11a piece to each fan, extending 1/2" onto the fan.
7. Add embroidery stitches and embellishments to the blocks.
8. Sew the blocks together in a straight set.
9. Attach mitered borders.
10. Cut the backing at least 1" larger than the quilt top all the way around.
11. With their right sides together, lay the backing and the quilt top on a smooth, flat surface.
12. Using glass-head pins, secure the layers around their edges.
13. Using a 1/4" seam, stitch the layers together leaving approximately a 12"–18" (depending on size) opening for turning.
14. Trim the backing even with the quilt top.
15. Turn the quilt right side out. Then hand stitch the opening closed.
16. With its top side facing up, lay the quilt on a smooth, flat surface. Pin and then baste the lace into position, centering it over the border and mitering at the corners.
17. Machine or hand stitch the lace to the quilt, stitching through all the layers.
18. With its backing side facing up, lay the quilt on a smooth, flat surface and tie with square knots to hold the layers in place.

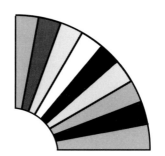

Step 1

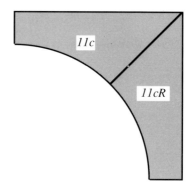

Step 2

CHAPTER 5

TRAPUNTO QUILTS

 Just the word "trapunto" makes many quiltmakers weak at the knees. It fills most of us with awesome fear. But the technique of trapunto is simple and can be easily mastered in a few hours of patient practice. Give trapunto a try.

Simply stated, trapunto is a method by which raised decoration can be added to any textile surface. Channels of parallel stitches or areas of patterned running stitches are filled to create the desired effect.

Trapunto is one of the oldest forms of textile decoration; examples exist from ancient Egypt, China and the Far East. There are even whole cloth trapunto quilts dating from 1400 A.D. that survive in Europe.

As a quiltmaker, you will find that trapunto is a wonderful way to dress up any quilt, from pieced to appliquéd. Trapunto always balances the strength of pieced or appliquéd work when placed in alternate blocks on a quilt. In addition, trapunto in those alternating blocks adds a new dimension that is most appealing. Both these features are readily apparent in Mary Helen Schwyn's beautiful quilt on page 126.

We hope you'll try your hand at making an heirloom trapunto quilt, but if thoughts of a bed-sized all-trapunto quilt seem overwhelming, put a little trapunto in your next quilt, to add another dimension to your creation.

TRAPUNTO FOR BLOCKS

SUPPLIES:

Front fabric: Medium-weight, solid fabric which is not too rough in texture. Avoid pima cotton, as it is too tightly woven and will pucker.

Inner-lining fabric: Batiste (cotton/polyester) in a color as close to your front fabric as possible.

Thread: 100% polyester (required for strength) in a color to match your front fabric. Do not use 100% cotton, as it will break: you will be doing a lot of pulling and tugging to keep the work flat and free of puckers. Also you will need a thin, light-colored basting thread.

Yarn: Inexpensive synthetic 4-ply. Look for a soft one in a color to match your front fabric. You can also use gift-wrap yarn: untwist it, so that you will be working with one separate ply at a time. Either can be found in your local variety store.

Needles: #10 or #12 Between for outlining the design, #20 tapestry for filling and 6″ blunt (soft-sculpture) needle for filling channels.

Fabric scissors

Small embroidery scissors

#3 lead pencil or silver artist's pencil

Glass-head pins

Tracing paper (at least 16″ × 16″)

Ultra-fine permanent pen

Pressing surface

Light-colored towel

Steam iron

Pinking shears (optional)

PREPARATION OF PATTERN

Using the ultra-fine permanent pen trace the entire pattern onto a piece of tracing paper. The larger trapunto patterns are presented in sections in the back of the book. For these patterns you must trace the sections from separate pages, aligning the sections to get the full pattern.

TRACING THE DESIGN ONTO FABRIC

1. Cut a piece of inner-lining fabric the desired size plus seam allowance. ✷ *Helpful hint:* Many fabrics will ravel badly while you are working with them. To preserve the edges, you can use pinking shears and cut a 1/2″ rather than the usual 1/4″ seam allowance. The excess can be trimmed off later. Remember to keep the lengthwise grainline consistent on all blocks. Use a pencil to mark the direction of the lengthwise grain in the seam allowance on the wrong side of each block.

2. Lay the traced pattern on a flat surface. With its right side facing up, center the inner-lining fabric over the traced pattern and secure it with glass-head pins.

3. Use your pencil to trace all lines onto the inner-lining fabric lightly.

4. Cut a piece of front fabric the same size as the inner-lining fabric. Refer to the helpful hint in Step 1 for preserving the edges of the fabric and marking the grainline.

5. With their right sides facing out, place the front fabric and the inner-lining fabrics together. Secure them with glass-head pins.

6. Use the basting thread and Between needle to baste the two layers together with a running stitch approximately 1/4″ from all edges. Baste in a 2″–3″ grid. These stitches will remain in the fabrics until the block is incorporated into the quilt.

✷ *Helpful hint:* Place the fabrics on a flat surface while basting to prevent them from shifting.

OUTLINING THE DESIGNS

1. Thread your Between needle with a single strand of polyester thread (approximately 18″–20″ long). Secure one end with a knot. ✷ *Helpful hint:* To avoid starting and stopping in the middle of a line, cut a length of thread at least as long as the marked line you wish to stitch.

2. With the marked side of the inner-lining fabric facing you, insert the needle into a line on the design and take a small backstitch through the inner-lining fabric only. The knots will show on this side, as all of your work will be done on this side of the inner-lining fabric. ✷ *Helpful hint:* It is generally a good idea to start in the center of the design and work outward.

3. Continue on the marked line with small running stitches, stitching through both thicknesses. Try to make the stitches as small as possible: small stitches will give a sharp definition to the design, whereas large

stitches will result in a wavy appearance. ✷ *Helpful hints:* a. Take a small backstitch at turning points before changing direction. This will give more definition and added strength. b. Take a small backstitch about every 1/2″ on long lines to keep the stitches in place and give added strength. c. At the end of a line (for example the vein of a leaf), take a small backstitch, then run the needle and thread between the two layers of fabric and bring them up on another line. If the distance between lines is more than 1/2″, it is better to end off the thread and re-start on the new line. d. Clip and remove the basting threads as you come to them. Do not sew over them. They will be too difficult to remove at a later time.

4. To end off your thread, take 2 or 3 small backstitches in place through the inner-lining fabric only. Then cut the thread.

5. Remove all remaining basting stitches except those made around the outer edges.

6. Press the fabrics on the inner-lining side and then the front fabric side.

INSERTING YARN

This step involves inserting yarn into the stitched designs, forming a raised design. As indicated in the supply list, the yarn should be a color as close to your front fabric as possible. All types of linear elements such as stems, tendrils and meandering vines which require two rows of stitching are called channels. Circles, flower petals, leaves and other larger spaces require more filling. For best results work from the center of the block out to the edges.

Filling Channels

1. Cut a 24″ length of yarn. Thread your needle with the yarn, finishing with a double strand 12″ in length. For narrow channels, use 4-ply yarn; for wide channels, use only one ply of gift wrap yarn. ✷ *Helpful hint:* Use a #20 tapestry needle for short or curved channels. Use a 6″ blunt needle for long, straight channels.

2. With the inner-lining fabric facing you, insert the needle at the end or at an angle of a channel, between the two layers of fabric and inside the stitching lines. Do not go through to the front fabric.

3. Run the needle through the channel from one end to the other, leaving approximately 1/8″ of yarn extending at the starting point.

4. Bring the needle and yarn out at the opposite end of the channel. Cut the yarn, leaving a 1/8″ tail.

5. Using both hands, tug on opposite ends of the stuffed channel to get the yarn in place and allow the cut ends to retract into the center of the stitched design. The yarn will be tight, especially if it has gone around a curve.

6. Insert the tip of the needle between the layers of fabric approximately 1/4″ from the end of a channel. Then, with the tip of the needle, work the yarn around to fill in the ends. This will keep the end of the design full and prevent it from going flat.

✷ *Helpful hint:* If you are working on a long channel or one which has sharp curves, run the needle and yarn as far as possible, leaving enough yarn to bring the needle through to the inner-lining side. Re-insert the needle into the same hole and continue in the same manner. If, however, the channel is longer than the length of yarn, run the needle and yarn as far as possible, then cut the yarn close to the fabric. Tug on the channel to allow the cut ends to retract into the center of the design. Then cut the new end' of yarn at an angle and re-insert the needle and yarn approximately 1/4″ behind the yarn end in the channel. The angled cut end will overlap the previously cut end, thereby preventing a gap in the channel.

7. With the tip of your needle, carefully work the threads to conceal the holes which you made at the beginning and end of the channel.

Filling Other Shapes

Design elements such as flower petals, leaves and circles require more yarn to fill their spaces. It is very important not to apply too much yarn to any one element and overfill it: that would cause the background around your design to pucker.

1. Cut a 24″ length of yarn. Thread your #20 tapestry needle with the yarn, finishing with a double strand 12″ in length.

2. For circles or flower centers, insert the needle between the layers of fabric (inside the stitching lines) on one side of the circle and bring it out on the opposite side. For petals or leaves, insert the needle at the tip of the design and run it lengthwise to the opposite end.

3. Cut the yarn, leaving a 1/8″ tail on each side.

4. Re-insert the needle alongside the first hole and bring it out at the opposite side. These strands of yarn will lie next to the first strands. Refer to the diagram and notice that you never go into or come out of the same hole twice, causing the yarn to lie over another strand. Keep the strands of yarn side by side. Make as many runs across the circle as necessary to fill the space and still maintain an unpuckered background.

5. Tug on opposite ends of the circle with both hands, allowing the 1/8″ yarn tails to retract to the center. If some of the ends still extend beyond the line, insert the tip of your needle into the circle and gently push the cut ends in.

6. With the tip of your needle, carefully work the threads to conceal the holes which you made at the beginning and end points of the shape.

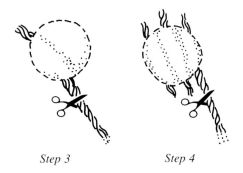

Step 3   Step 4

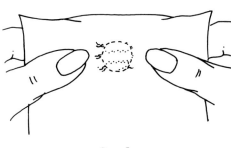

Step 5

BLOCKING

This next step is important, as your block will be out of shape because of the tugging required when you inserted the yarn.

1. Lay your block flat on a board which can be pinned into.

2. Place pins every 1/2″ around all edges to keep the block straight and hold it taut.

3. With your iron set on steam, hold the iron approximately 1/2″ above the block, allowing the steam to penetrate the fabric. *Do not* allow the iron to touch the block.

4. Let the block dry completely before removing the pins.

5. The block is ready to be used in your quilt.

TRAPUNTO FOR WHOLE CLOTH QUILTS

SUPPLIES:

Front and backing fabrics: Medium-weight, solid fabric which is not too rough in texture. Avoid pima cotton, as it is too tightly woven and will pucker. Choose a weight which will easily accept the yarn and tapestry needle. The front and backing fabrics should be the same color.

Thread: 100% polyester (required for strength) in a color to match your front fabric. Do not use 100% cotton, as it will break: you will be doing a lot of pulling and tugging to keep the work flat and free of puckers. Also you will need a thin, light-colored basting thread.

Yarn: Inexpensive synthetic 4-ply. Look for a soft one in a color to match your fabric. You can also use gift-wrap yarn: untwist it, so that you will be working with one separate ply at a time. Either can be found in your local variety store.

Needles: #10 or #12 Between for outlining the design, #20 tapestry for filling and 6″ blunt (soft-sculpture) needle for filling channels.

Fabric scissors

Small embroidery scissors

#3 lead pencil or silver artist's pencil

Glass-head pins

Tracing paper

Ultra-fine permanent pen

Drafting tape

Thin, light-colored paper or tracing paper used for flat pattern making

Steam iron

Light-colored towel

Transferring supplies: see Chapter Six

Sewing machine (optional)

Pinking shears (optional)

Batting, thin (optional)

Trapunto is especially suitable for whole cloth quilts. It can be done with or without a batting layer. The majority of older trapunto quilts were made without batting. However, a very thin batting layer can be included if you desire a fuller look. It will be necessary to make the quilting stitches close together to avoid a puffy look. Also, it will be more difficult to keep the stitches outlining the designs very small, as there will be the additional batting layer to work through.

1. Prepare your backing fabric; sew lengths together if necessary.

2. Lightly mark the design onto the right side of the backing fabric.
✳ *Helpful hint:* Use one of the techniques for transferring designs to fabric described in Chapter Six.

3. With their wrong sides together, layer the front and the backing fabrics. If a batting is used, place it between the two fabrics.

4. Hand baste the fabrics together with long running stitches in a 2″–3″ grid. Then, hand baste around the entire quilt 1/4″ from the edge.

5. With the right side of the backing fabric facing you, use your small Between needle and polyester thread to stitch around the marked designs. Refer to Steps 1 through 6 of "Outlining the Designs" above for specific instructions.

6. Apply yarn to the designs. Refer to the sections on "Filling Channels" and "Filling Other Shapes" for specific instructions.

7. Block the quilt. Blocking is done in sections. You can place a large towel on the floor or carpet, pin the quilt in place to straighten the edges, and then steam. Allow it to dry completely before moving it.

8. Your quilt top is now ready to be marked with quilting lines and quilted if you desire.

PRACTICE EXERCISE: Making an 8″ block. Use Template 15a.

This pattern was designed by Adele Ingraham and the following technique is taught by her. We feel that it is a good first exercise because of its short channels and small, delicate shapes. If you can master this one you are ready to attempt any one of the other trapunto designs contained in this book.

1. Use the ultra-fine permanent pen to trace the design onto the tracing paper.

2. Use your pencil to trace all lines lightly onto the inner-lining fabric.

3. Layer, pin and then baste the inner-lining fabric and the front fabric together. See Steps 5 and 6 of "Tracing the Design onto Fabric" for help.

4. Using your Between needle and polyester thread, stitch on all marked lines with small running stitches. See Steps 1 through 6 of "Outlining the Designs" for help. Remember: clip and remove basting threads as you come to them.

5. Using your tapestry needle and a double strand, insert yarn into the channels. See the helpful hint in Step 6 of "Filling Channels" for help.

6. Fill the four circles (two flower centers and two attached to the ends of channels) with yarn. Fill the flowers and the leaves with yarn, referring to the diagrams. See "Filling Other Shapes" for help.

7. Remove all remaining basting threads except those made around the outer edge.

8. Lay the completed design on a flat board and use your iron to block it into shape. See "Blocking" for help.

This completes the practice exercise for trapunto.

ORIENTAL FLORAL BOUQUET

Designed and made by Adele Ingraham

An original design by Adele Ingraham

Techniques: Trapunto and whole cloth
Fabric suggestions: Cotton, cotton sateen, cotton/polyester.

If you wish to copy this quilt precisely, a full-size pattern can be purchased directly from Adele Ingraham, 204 Dundee Way, Benicia, CA 94510.

	Crib/Wall
Finished size	42″ × 54″

YARDAGE

	Crib/Wall
Front fabric (includes binding)	2
Backing	1⅝

CONSTRUCTION

1. Create or choose your own trapunto patterns. Then trace and enlarge them (if necessary) to a full-size paper pattern.

2. Trace your designs onto fabric. See "Tracing the Design Onto Fabric."

3. Outline the designs with your quilting stitch. See "Outlining the Designs."

4. Insert yarn into the designs. See "Filling Channels" and "Filling Other Shapes."

5. Block your quilt. See Step 7 of "Trapunto for Whole-Cloth Quilts."

6. Bind your quilt.

CALIFORNIA SUNSET

An original pattern by Jinny Beyer

Block size: 15″
Techniques: Quick cutting or Templates 1c, 1f, 1i, 3n, 7e *and* Templates 6c, 7b, 7c, 7d and trapunto Template 13a
Setting: Straight
Fabric Suggestions: Light background and seven fabrics for pieced blocks and border.

This is an original setting. Yardage is given for one size only.

	King
Finished size	112″ × 99″
Blocks set	5 × 5
# pieced blocks	13
# trapunto blocks	12

YARDAGE

	King
Light background	7
Template 1f	¼
Template 3n, light and medium, *each*	⅜
Template 7e (includes binding)	2
Template 7c, medium and light, *each*	½
Templates 7c and 7d, light	1½
Template 7b and borders	3½
Template 6c	1
Backing	9

CUTTING

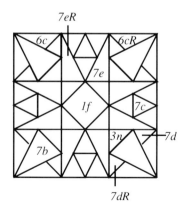

	King
Light background:	
Borders: One at:	6″ × 78″
Three at:	12½″ × 110″
Trapunto blocks:	
number of 16″ squares	12
Sawtooth borders:	
Template 1i	308
— OR —	
Quick: number of strips*	10
Template 1c	4
— OR —	
Quick: number of strips	1
Prints:	
Template 1f	13
— OR —	
Quick: number of strips	2

Template 3n, light and medium, *each*	52
— OR —	
Quick: number of strips, *each*	3
Template 7e	52 and 52R
— OR —	
Quick: number of strips	4
Template 7c:	
Light fabric	104
— OR —	
Quick: number of strips	7
and	
Medium and dark fabrics, *each*	52
— OR —	
Quick: number of strips, *each*	4
Template 7d	52 and 52R
— OR —	
Quick: number of strips	7
Template 7b	52
— OR —	
Quick: number of strips	4
Template 6c	52 and 52R
— OR —	
Quick: number of strips	12
Dark solid borders:	
Inside—width:	1½″
Outside—width:	2¼″
Sawtooth borders:	
Template 1i	308
— OR —	
Quick: number of strips*	10
Backing: number of lengths	3

*Or use the grid method of making half-square triangles.

  R = reverse template on fabric.

Quick cutting: Cut all of your quilt top fabrics (except borders) crossgrain.
- For 1f: Cut 4″-wide strips. Then cut to 4″ squares.
- For 3n: Cut 3⅜″-wide strips. Then cut to 3⅜″ squares. Cut each square in *half diagonally.*
- For 7e & 7eR: Cut 6¼″-wide strips. Then cut to 3⅛″ × 6¼″ rectangles. Cut each rectangle in *half diagonally.*
- For 7c: Cut 3¼″-wide strips. Then use template to mark and cut angles.
- For 7d and 7dR: Cut 3⅛″-wide strips. Then use template to mark and cut angles.
- For 7b: Cut 6⅜″-wide strips. Then use template to mark and cut angles.
- For 6c and 6cR: Cut 2¼″-wide strips. Then use template to mark and cut angles.
- For 1c: Cut 2¼″-wide strips. Then cut to 2¼″ squares.
- For 1i: Cut 2⅝″-wide strips. Then cut to 2⅝″ squares. Cut each square in *half diagonally.*

CONSTRUCTION

Pieced blocks:
  1. Make the following units, exactly as shown in the diagrams.

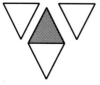

Step 1

Step 2

2. Sew order (see diagram).

Trapunto blocks:

Make the required number of trapunto blocks using Template 13a. Refer to this chapter for help with techniques.

Solid borders:

Attach border strips. Trim off excess length.

Sawtooth borders:

1. Use one of the methods for making the half-square triangle units, using the light and dark Template 1i pieces.

2. Attach the pieced border strips to the quilt top. The Template 1c squares are the corners of the pieced borders.

Made by Mary Helen Schwyn from a Jinny Beyer pattern, with her own trapunto designs

CHAPTER 6

WHOLE CLOTH QUILTS

 Even many experienced quilters despair at the thought of creating a whole cloth quilt where their quilting stitches will be highlighted and exposed to the critical light of day. Yet creating a whole cloth quilt can be a liberating experience for any quiltmaker.

Take the time to plan and execute a whole cloth quilt and you will end up a much better (and more relaxed) quilter than when you started—regardless of your current proficiency at plying a needle through cloth. Hand quilting is a soothing, rejuvenating experience for both of us, and we hope that you will try your hand at it.

If you are new to quilting, your initial stitches will probably feel awkward and unsure, and the process will be slow. In part this may result from trying to manipulate a very small needle through two thicknesses of fabric and a layer of batting while using a thimble for the first time. If you are like most novice quilters, your reward for all this technically difficult and precise work will be uneven stitches. Do not despair. Do not be discouraged. As with any technical and precise motor skill, practice makes perfect. It takes time, effort and work to master the simple quilting stitch. But there is hope. We have found that, if you allow yourself about three hours of uninterrupted quiet time to practice this stitch calmly, eventually all the different parts come together smoothly and easily as you hit your stride. You will not so much know that this has happened as feel it. You will now be able to complete well-made and proper stitches with a comfortable rhythm. Do not be overly concerned at this time about the length of your stitches. Instead, concentrate on being sure that the spacing of your stitches is uniform and even. In time, as you gain experience and confidence, your stitches will become smaller and more precise. Eventually they will begin to look like the fine stitches you have admired on heirloom quilts. This is your reward for practice and perseverance.

MAKING YOUR WHOLE CLOTH QUILT

SUPPLIES:

Fabric: 100% cotton, cotton/ polyester, silk or wool. Fabrics which have a sheen, such as a polished cotton or cotton sateen, are especially attractive; the raised areas catch the light, thereby enhancing the quilting. ✷ *Helpful hint:* Some fabrics come as wide as 108″; therefore, no piecing is required.

Thread: Cotton-covered polyester, extra strong hand quilting – *OR* – extra strong quilting cotton – *OR* –any dressmaking thread used with beeswax. Other thread such as perle cotton or buttonhole twist can be used, although a larger needle such as a #5 or #7 will be required to accommodate the thickness. The color need not match the fabric. It can be a shade lighter or darker or a contrasting color. Generally, a thin thread produces a stitch which embeds into the fabric, giving texture, whereas a thick thread produces a more decorative stitch which is raised on the top of the fabric. A thin, light-colored thread is needed for basting.

Marking pencil: An artist's silver pencil works well on both light and dark fabrics. Berol Prisma-color pencils and Caran D'Ache #2 water-soluble pencils come in a variety of colors and work well for marking the quilting line.

Batting: Cotton, cotton/polyester or polyester. Generally, packaged batting will produce better results than that purchased by the yard, as it is of better quality. Some battings sold by the yard are designed for craft and uphol-stery projects and are unsuitable for whole cloth quilts, as they are too stiff and wiry. Also, packaged batting comes in various sizes, so you may not have to piece lengths together. Select a good-quality batting which is smooth (without lumps), airy and not too thick (1/4″ or less). If possible, look for one which resists fiber migration. A light-weight batting gives a flatter, more traditional look and

SELECTING THE QUILTING DESIGNS

Lucy Hilty, an expert on whole cloth quilts, tells us that the design is the most important aspect of a whole cloth quilt. It should be strong and yet simple, be well-organized, maintain unity and rhythm. Most people have a tendency to choose too many motifs and try to incorporate them into one quilt. It is best not to use too many unrelated motifs, but rather choose one design and repeat it, or elements from it.

There are many plastic quilting templates and pattern books which have beautiful quilting designs appropriate for a whole cloth quilt. Or you may choose to create your own designs. Keep in mind the overall size of your quilt when looking for quilting designs. Proportion is just as important as the design.

MAKING A PAPER PATTERN

This next step is time-consuming, but we feel it solves many design problems and gives you an opportunity to view the entire design.

1. You may find it helpful to make a small sketch of your overall design onto a piece of graph paper.

2. Using large pieces of tracing paper or thin, light-colored paper, tape several pieces together, if necessary, to obtain the desired size of your quilt. ✷ *Helpful hint:* There is 1″ gridded paper which is designed for flat pattern making which works extremely well for this process. You should be able to purchase it at your local fabric store.

3. Use the ultra-fine permanent pen to mark the center both horizon-tally and vertically. Divide the area further into sections of quarters or eighths (depending upon the size). Then fold the paper pattern to obtain diagonal lines. These guide lines will be helpful when arranging the designs.

4. If you are using plastic quilting templates, you can experiment with different arrangements, laying the templates on top of the paper pattern. Stand back to study the overall design to see that the individual designs are in good proportion to the overall pattern. This is the time to make any changes so that the motifs work well together. If you do a center design, check to see if the design is too small for the center. The place-ment of the motifs can affect the balance, so try out various sizes and shapes until you feel good about the motif designs on paper. Now that you have put all the design motifs on your paper, take a look and check two points that may lead to a successful whole cloth quilt. Are the motifs too small or too large? Do the motifs relate to each other? When you are satisfied with the placement of the designs, use the permanent pen to mark the designs onto the paper. ✷ *Helpful hint:* If your overall design is symmetrical, it is only necessary to trace one-quarter of the design.

— *OR* —

If you have made your own quilting templates on tracing paper, place a heavier, thicker batting requires more quilting; otherwise, the quilt will be puffy.

Needle: #9, 10 or 12 Between. The higher the number, the smaller the needle.

Quilting designs or templates

Quilting hoop or frame

Thimble

Small embroidery scissors

Needle grabber or piece of balloon

Black ultra-fine permanent pen

Cotton darning needle, #1

Masking tape

Large C-Thru ruler

Fabric scissors – OR –

Rotary cutter

Sewing machine

Steam iron

Pressing surface

Light-colored towel

Supplies for transferring designs to fabric:
   Tracing paper or thin, light-colored paper – OR –
   Tracing wheel with tracing paper and cutting board – OR –
   Plexiglas and lamp

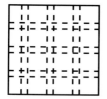 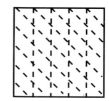

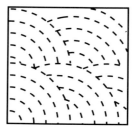

the marked designs underneath the paper pattern in a pleasing arrangement; since the paper is light-colored, you can easily see the designs to mark onto the paper.

5. Make any adjustments on your paper pattern before transferring the markings to your fabric.

BACKGROUND FILLING

After your designs have been arranged onto the paper pattern, stand back and look at the designs themselves (positive space) and the space around the designs (negative space), which is called the background. This negative space is just as important in whole cloth quilting as the designs themselves. If you fill up all the background space with too many designs, you may find your planned quilt is too busy and confusing. Your quilting designs will become lost. If, on the other hand, you leave too much background space, the designs will not have much importance and will seem to float in space.

The background space needs to be filled with quilting lines that complement your design motif. These lines help to unify the entire quilt. The background filler lines make your primary designs stand out. Go back to your paper pattern and determine filling patterns that will successfully enhance your motifs. It is not necessary that you spend the time to fill in all of the background quilting lines on the paper pattern. They can be marked directly onto the fabric.

TRANSFERRING DESIGNS TO FABRIC

If a quilt size larger than the width of your fabric is desired, purchase two or more lengths. If two or more lengths are required, cut the selvage edges off the lengths and stitch them together along the longer sides with a 1/4″ seam. Press the seam(s) open. ✷ *Helpful hint:* Seams are stronger when pressed to one side; however, if your fabric is thin and/or light-colored, you may want to press the seam open to avoid a darker streak down the center of your quilt top. This open seam will also be easier to quilt through.

Your quilt top fabric should be at least 1″ larger than the desired finished size all the way around. With a long hand running stitch, mark the center of the quilt top both horizontally and vertically.

Three methods for transferring the design from the paper pattern to the fabric are given below. Read through them carefully and choose the one that is appropriate for your quilt.

Method One — Overlaying Pattern

If you are using a light-colored fabric, you can simply lay the fabric over the paper pattern and trace.

1. With the right side facing up, tape your paper pattern taut to a smooth flat surface.

2. With the right side facing up, lay your fabric over the paper pattern, lining up the center marks on the fabric with those on the paper pattern.

Tape it in place around the edges.

3. With your marking pencil, trace around all of the designs with a thin, light line.

Method Two — Dressmaker's Tracing Paper

If your fabric is too dark to use Method One, you can use dressmaker's tracing paper and a tracing wheel for ease in transferring the pattern. The dressmaker's tracing paper and tracing wheel will allow you to transfer the pattern markings from the pattern to the fabric. The tracing paper comes in a variety of colors. Choose a color close to (but not the same as) your fabric color rather than a contrasting color. For example, use a yellow tracing paper on white fabric. Test the tracing paper on a scrap of your fabric before transferring the entire design. The markings can be removed from the fabric by washing *before* pressing. ◨ *Warning:* Wash the scrap to test for mark removal.

1. With the right side facing up, tape your fabric taut to a smooth, flat surface. ✷ *Helpful hint:* Use a piece of cardboard or cutting board under the area to be traced for clearer markings.

2. With the waxy side face down, place a piece of dressmaker's tracing paper at the center of the quilt top.

3. With the marked side face up, lay the paper pattern over the fabric and tracing paper, lining up the center markings with the running stitches on the fabric. Use a few pieces of tape to secure it, leaving enough space along the sides to reach under and re-position the dressmaker's tracing paper when necessary.

4. Run a tracing wheel over the marked lines within the area of the tracing paper. Apply only enough pressure to produce a light, visible marking.

5. Re-position the dressmaker's tracing paper and use the wheel to continue tracing the design.

6. Continue moving the dressmaker's tracing paper until all of the marked lines have been transferred to the fabric. ✷ *Helpful hint:* Use your large C-Thru ruler against the tracing wheel as a guide for transferring straight lines.

Method Three — Light Table

Another option for tracing onto darker fabrics is to make your own light table.

1. Use a glass table or place a piece of Plexiglas over a dining table which has been opened for insertion of its extension leaves.

2. Place a lamp underneath the glass or Plexiglas.

3. Place the pattern on the glass or Plexiglas and the fabric over the pattern.

4. Use the marking pencil to trace lightly onto the fabric.

PREPARING THE BACKING

The backing fabric should be at least 2″ larger than the quilt top all around. Layer the backing, batting and quilt top. If you will be quilting in a hoop, baste the three layers together with a long diagonal basting stitch. If you will be using a frame, follow the instructions which accompany your frame.

QUILTING

Either a hoop or a quilting frame is recommended, because either will help with the tension of the stitches. It is easier to manipulate the stitches if the fabric is spongy like a marshmallow. The tension must be neither too tight nor too loose. An even tension is important becasue it creates the illusion of even stitches. If the tension is too loose, the stitches will not embed into the fabric to produce valleys; if the tension is too tight, the stitches will cause the fabric to pucker.

Another reason for using a hoop or frame is that it allows the hand that makes the stitches to be free rather than having to hold onto the fabric. Practice with different degrees of tension so you can see the different effects. ◨ *Warning:* Overhandling your quilt can cause some of the marked lines to disappear.

As we've stated, it takes time to learn the quilting stitch, but practice does make perfect. Start with an 18″–22″ length of thread. When quilting, rhythm is important. Use a rocking motion: down-up-down-up-down-up, picking up about four stitches on the tip of your needle at a time.

Stipple Quilting

These stitches are worked tightly together, constricting the batting, to give the area a stipple effect. This is best used in small areas for giving decorative interest to the quilting design. We do not recommend using this as an overall background filling stitch.

Steps 1-4

1. Stitch on the outline of the design.

2. Stitch 1/16″ outside this line. This line of stitching gives more definition to the outline of the design.

3. The next row of stitches is made 1/8″ out from the previous row, going in the opposite direction.

4. The next and following rows are made 1/8″ apart, alternating the direction. Notice from the diagram that stitches are alternate or offset rather than lined up vertically.

✷ *Helpful hint:* If the space you wish to fill with stipple quilting is large, it is better to divide it into smaller spaces. You may also use stipple quilting inside a design shape.

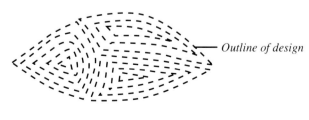

— *Outline of design*

Helpful Hint

WHOLE CLOTH

Designed and made by Shirley A. Shenk

Technique: Hand quilting
Quilting stencils: Feathered plume, small feather border, corner decorative floral, large feather border with corner piece.
Fabric suggestions: Smooth, even weave cotton or cotton sateen in light, medium or dark solid colors.

	Crib	Twin	Double	Queen	King
Suggested finished size	42″ × 58″	67″ × 89″	81″ × 89″	88″ × 94″	100″ × 98″

YARDAGE

	Crib	Twin	Double	Queen	King
Front fabric (includes binding)	2⅛	5¾	6	9	9¼
Backing	1¾	5¼	5¼	8¼	8½

CUTTING

	Crib	Twin	Double	Queen	King
Front and backing fabric, number of lengths, *each*	1	2	2	3	3

Plastic quilting stencils are readily available at quilt shops throughout the country. Therefore, we have given you this quilt to inspire your own choice of quilting designs. We recommend that you purchase a feathered plume, a feathered border with its accompanying corner template and a decorative floral spray. You can use these plastic quilting templates for designing your quilt on paper before placing the markings on your fabric.

Templates can be purchased by mail order from Smith Quilting Stencils, P.O. Box 3429, Kingman, AZ 86402.

CHAPTER 7

STENCILED QUILTS

SUPPLIES:

Fabric: Small print or solid:
muslin, broadcloth or sheeting.
Light to medium colors work
best.

Stencil brushes: 1/4″–3/4″ are
adequate for almost any project.

Textile paint

Mylar or clear acetate (.005) or
waxed stencil paper

Tracing paper—for large patterns
only

Lead pencil

Masking tape

Cutting surface (sheet of glass—
approximately 10″ × 10″)

Black ultra-fine permanent pen

X-Acto knife with #11 blade

Paper plate

Plastic spoons

Cellophane tape

Piece of non-corrugated cardboard

Pressing surface

Light-colored towel

Iron

Pressing cloth or piece of muslin

Fabric scissors – *OR* **–**

Rotary cutter

Ruler

 If you've never tried your hand at stenciling, we urge you to do so. It's simple, easy and fun. And there is not nearly the mess that you might envision. Stenciling products today are of a high quality and your color palette is virtually unlimited.

Stenciled quilts enjoyed considerable popularity in America between 1815 and 1850. Influenced by stenciled home products (Boston rockers, Hitchcock chairs) and the work of itinerant stencil artists who traveled from village to town, stenciling the walls, furniture and floors of entire households at a time, women produced stenciled quilts of great variety and beauty. Most were, in fact, spreads of heavy cloth, left unquilted because of the weight of the fabric employed in their production. Botanical themes predominated, and birds and small animals were often depicted. Sometimes, stenciled motifs resembled the pieced patterns (like stars) being used by quiltmakers.

By 1850, American industry was producing a wide array of household decorating products, such as printed wallpaper. As a result, stenciling, like many other folk art forms, disappeared.

We include stenciled quilts here because stenciling gives you another versatile technique that expands your quiltmaking repertoire. For example, any stencil pattern can also be used in appliqué or quilting, or vice versa. Because stencils are permanent, once they are produced they can be stored away and brought out to be used again on future projects. And, since stencils can be flopped over to reverse the design motif, a stencil actually gives you two designs with which to work.

Look at our stenciled examples (pages 140, 144, 155). In Ren Brown and Laura's quilt on page 144, a simple stenciled leaf motif has been joined to the pieced pattern. Here a stencil is being used to diffuse the bold contrasts and colors of the pieced design.

Ren Brown has taken one of Adele Ingraham's appliqué patterns and adapted it for stenciling in her beautiful rendition of the *Heart Wreath* on page 140.

Use our stencil designs in your quilts, adding them to alternate blocks, border strips or corners. And create some of your own. Use patterns you see and like in wallpapers, fabrics or other media as your inspirations. By mastering the art of stenciling, you will add a considerable asset to your quiltmaking repertoire.

PREPARATION OF PATTERN

The stencil patterns in the back of the book are given in full size. Due to the size limitations of this book, the larger patterns are presented in sections. For these patterns you must trace the sections from separate pages, aligning the sections to get the full pattern.

These next few steps are required only for the large patterns, as the small patterns can be traced directly onto the mylar from the book.

1. Lay the top section of a piece of tracing paper over the top section of the stencil pattern found in the back of the book.

2. Using the ultra-fine permanent pen, copy the design onto the tracing paper, numbering the shapes 1, 2, 3, etc., as shown on the pattern. You will also need to mark any center-line dots and corners.

3. Repeat Steps 1 and 2 for the other sections of the pattern, making sure the design lines up at all meeting points.

TRACING THE DESIGN

Stencil 1

Step 3

As indicated in this chapter's supply list, mylar, clear acetate (.005) or waxed stencil paper is acceptable for this next step. For purposes of instruction, we will be referring to it as mylar; the procedures are identical for all three materials.

Each stencil pattern included in this book will require making two or more mylar stencils. Remember, each shape of the stencil pattern is given a number (1, 2, 3, etc.) indicating the stencil it should be traced onto. General tracing instructions follow. Refer to the individual patterns for more details.

1. Cut a piece of mylar at least 1″ larger than the stencil pattern on all sides. Then position the mylar over the stencil pattern, leaving a 1″ allowance on all sides. This 1″ margin keeps the brush from smudging over the edges of the stencil. Secure this with masking tape.

2. Use your black ultra-fine permanent pen to make dots (called registration marks) around each corner. These marks will later be used to align the stencil with the raw edges of the fabric.

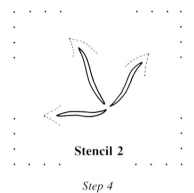

Stencil 2

Step 4

3. Next, carefully trace around all of the number 1 shapes. Then label this stencil 1, exactly as shown in the diagram.

4. If more than one stencil is required, repeat Steps 2 and 3 for each, tracing all of the shapes numbered 2 onto stencil 2 and all of the shapes numbered 3 onto stencil 3, etc. In order to overlay these stencils accurately, make a few registration marks around some of the number 1 shapes onto stencils 2 and 3, exactly as shown in the diagram.

CUTTING THE STENCILS

Be patient with this procedure, as it does take practice!

1. Lay the mylar on top of the sheet of glass.

2. Holding the X-Acto knife as you would a pencil, press the blade *very hard* into the mylar and, with one continuous cut rather than lifting the blade, cut around the marked lines. Cut as accurately as possible to avoid overlapping or gaps in overlaying the stencils. This technique can be achieved more easily if you try to rotate the mylar with your free hand instead of raising and lowering the blade. Remember, try not to lift the cutting blade; instead, continue turning the stencil so you will always be cutting toward yourself. Your goal is a smoothly cut edge. ◘ *Warning:* If you hear any popping sounds, or if you are tugging on the X-Acto knife, you need a new blade. *Do not* cut on any of the registration marks. These are used only for ease in overlaying stencils.

✱ *Helpful hints:* An angled area, rather than the center of a curved edge, makes a good starting point. Cut small detail areas first to avoid weakening the stencil. If the mylar should tear, use the cellophane tape to mend the tear, then continue cutting.

3. Repeat Steps 1 and 2 for each required stencil.

PREPARATION OF FABRIC

1. Pre-wash your fabric in warm water (no detergent) to remove the sizing.

2. Cut the fabric along the straight grain in pieces the required sizes (for blocks, sashing, borders, etc.). Be sure to include seam allowance.

— OR —

Rather than cutting your piece of fabric into smaller pieces, determine the straight grain of the fabric and use a lead pencil to mark the required sizes onto the fabric. For example, if you are making the *Twenty-five Patch* on page 144, you can simply mark a 5½" grid onto the right side of the fabric. You can stencil all of the leaves, then cut the blocks apart.

APPLYING THE PAINT

1. Lay your piece of cardboard on a flat surface. The piece of cardboard should be larger than the area which will be stenciled.

2. With its right side facing up, lay the fabric on top of the cardboard.

3. Position stencil 1 on top of the fabric, aligning the corner registration marks with the corners of the fabric. Secure it with masking tape.

4. Use a plastic spoon to stir the paint if necessary; some brands may tend to separate in the jar. Then use the plastic spoon to scoop some of the textile paint onto a paper plate. Use additional spoons to add additional colors if you will be blending colors. Mix thoroughly. ✷ *Helpful hint:* Add a small amount of black to cool colors and a small amount of brown to warm colors in order to achieve a deeper, darker tone. Add a small amount of white to the color for a lighter tint. Mix 2–3 tablespoons to be sure there is enough to complete your project. You can store any excess in a small jar with a resealable lid, such as a baby-food jar.

For best results, make a trial sample. If you are trying to match the paint to your fabric palette, you can tape small swatches of your fabrics to a piece of paper, lining them one under the other. Tape a larger swatch

of your background fabric directly next to the small swatches. Experiment with paint samples onto the background fabric and directly next to the fabric you wish to match.

5. When you are satisfied with the color, dip the flat end of your stencil brush into the paint. Avoid getting any paint onto the sides of the bristles.

6. Dab most of the paint off onto a clean area of the plate. There should be *very little* paint on the brush. ✷ *Helpful hint:* If the brush has recently been washed, you must wait 24 hours before using it for best results, or you can use a hair dryer for fast drying. A wet brush will moisten the fabric and cause the paint to bleed.

7. Working from the cut edge of a shape inward, firmly pounce the brush onto the fabric, keeping the flat end perpendicular to the fabric to avoid forcing paint under the cut edge of the stencil. The more you pounce in one area, the darker it will become. ✷ *Helpful hint:* To achieve the effect of a light source and a more realistic look, keep the area onto which the most light would fall lighter than the rest of the design. For example, a light source coming from overhead would result in a lighter center, whereas a light source coming from the left would result in a lighter left side.

8. When you have finished all shapes of stencil 1, release the stencil at the taped areas first, to avoid tearing at any weak spots.

9. If the paint finish appears dull, you are ready to overlay the painted design with the next stencil. A shiny finish indicates it is still wet, and you should wait a few minutes before proceeding.

10. Repeat Steps 3–9 for stencils 2, 3, 4, etc., each time being careful to keep the registration marks lined up.

✷ *Helpful hint:* One brush can be used if you first stencil all blocks with the same color. Otherwise, you will need additional brushes. If you must stop and start, your brush should be tightly wrapped in a plastic bag or plastic wrap to prevent the paint from air-drying. Do not wash the brush; if you do, you must wait 24 hours to use it again.

HEAT SETTING

Wait at least 15 minutes between painting and heat setting to be sure that the paint is completely dry. The instructions which accompany your individual brand of textile paints will specify the minimum drying time.

1. With the right side facing up, place the painted fabric on your pressing surface. Cover with a pressing cloth or piece of muslin.

2. Use a dry iron (no steam, with all the water removed to avoid any leaks which will cause the paint to run) with a temperature setting appropriate for the fiber content of your fabric. Press for the length of time recommended by your particular brand of paints.

3. Your blocks are now completed and ready to be included in your quilt.

CLEAN-UP

1. Wash the stencils and the brushes in warm, soapy water. Use the brushes to clean the paint gently from the stencils. Note that the waxed stencil paper is not washable.

2. Wash the brushes until the rinse water runs clear. Then blot them and let them dry flat.

3. Store the brushes flat or with the bristles up. Store the stencils flat in a file folder to prevent them from curling or bending.

SUPPLIES:
5½" square of light-colored fabric for background
Black ultra-fine permanent pen
Mylar
X-Acto knife
Glass cutting surface
Masking tape
Stencil brushes
Textile paint
Plastic spoons
Paper plate
Pressing surface
Pressing cloth
Iron

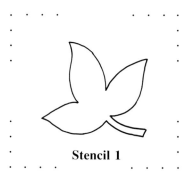

Stencil 1

Step 1

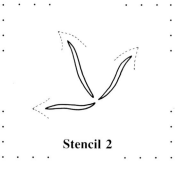

Stencil 2

Step 2

PRACTICE EXERCISE: For making a 5" *Leaf* block.

Use Template 16a.

1. Two stencils are required for this design. Use an ultra-fine permanent pen to trace all of the number 1 shapes onto a piece of mylar. Be sure to include corner registration marks and to label this stencil 1, exactly as shown in the diagram.

2. Trace all of the number 2 shapes onto another piece of mylar. Be sure to include corner registration marks as well as a few marks around some of the number 1 shapes for ease in overlaying. Label this stencil 2, exactly as shown in the diagram.

3. Use an X-Acto knife and glass cutting surface to cut all of the shapes from both stencils.

4. Lay stencil 1 over the right side of the fabric, aligning the corner registration marks with the raw edges of the fabric. Secure it with tape.

5. Apply paint to the number 1 shapes.

6. When the paint is dry, carefully remove the stencil.

7. Lay stencil 2 over the fabric, lining up the registration marks.

8. Apply paint to all the number 2 shapes. ✷ *Helpful hint:* Add a small amount of black paint to your leaf color to achieve a darker color for the veins.

9. Carefully remove stencil 2 and, when the paint is dry, heat set the design.

This completes the practice exercise for stenciling.

Additional Reading Material

Bishop, Adele, and Cile Lord. *The Art of Decorative Stenciling.* New York: The Viking Press, 1976.

Pettit, Florence H. *America's Printed and Painted Fabrics, 1600–1900.* New York: Hastings House, 1970.

HEART WREATH

Design by Adele Ingraham, adapted and stenciled by Ren Brown and made by Diana McClun

Block size: 15″
Techniques: Stenciling (Templates 21a, 22a, 23a, 24a, 25a, 26a and 26b)
Setting: Straight
Fabric suggestions: Light-colored cotton or sateen.

	Crib/Wall	Twin	Double/Queen	King
Finished size	45″ × 45″	65″ × 85″	85″ × 85″	105″ × 105″
Blocks set	2 × 2	3 × 4	4 × 4	5 × 5
Total blocks	4	12	16	25

YARDAGE

	Crib/Wall	Twin	Double/Queen	King
Front fabric (includes binding)	2½	4½	6¼	9½
Backing	2¾	5	7½	9¼

NOTE: Extra yardage is required if using sateen. All pieces should be cut so that the lengthwise grain is consistent when joined.

CUTTING

	Crib/Wall	Twin	Double/Queen	King
Borders:				
Two for Sides A at:	5½″ × 39″	5½″ × 79″	5½″ × 79″	5½″ × 99″
Two for Sides B at:	5½″ × 39″	5½″ × 59″	5½″ × 79″	5½″ × 99″
Blocks: number of 15½″ squares	4	12	16	25
Sashing: number of 5½″ × 15½″ pieces	4	17	24	40
Posts: number of 5½″ squares	5	10	13	20
Backing: number of lengths	2	2	3	3

CONSTRUCTION

1. Stencil the required number of blocks. Use Templates 21a, 22a, 23a and 24a (four stencils required for this design). Notice that the leaves are divided in half, half numbered Stencil 1 and the other half Stencil 4. Ren suggests cutting the entire leaf shape onto Stencil 1 and only that portion marked with the number 4 onto Stencil 4. Apply a light shade of paint to the entire Stencil 1 shape and then a darker color to the Stencil 4 portion. This technique will avoid a gap in the common line of 1 and 4. ✷ *Helpful hint:* The six colors Ren used on this beautiful quilt are: cranberry, rose, light teal, dark teal, navy and medium green.

2. Stencil the required number of sashing strips, using Template 25a. Notice that you will have to join the two sections, using the registration marks to achieve the full design. Three stencils are required.

3. Stencil the border strips, using Template 26a. Three stencils are required. Begin 2″ from the left-hand edge of each strip to allow for trimming.

4. Stencil four corner posts, using Template 26b.

5. Join the blocks to the sashing strips and posts.

6. Attach the borders (trimming excess length) and corner posts.

TWENTY-FIVE PATCH

Block One

Block Two

Block size: 5″
Grid category: Five Patch
Techniques: Quick cutting or Templates 1r, 5b and 8b and Stencil Template 16a.
NOTE: The leaf design can also be appliquéd.
Setting: Straight
Fabric Suggestions: Light for leaf blocks and a variety of fabrics for pieced blocks. Border to complement your quilt top.

	Crib/Wall	Twin	Double	Queen	King
Finished size	43″ × 53″	73″ × 93″	83″ × 93″	93″ × 93″	103″ × 103″
Blocks set	7 × 9	13 × 17	15 × 17	17 × 17	19 × 19
# pieced blocks	32	110	128	144	180
# stenciled blocks	31	111	127	145	181

YARDAGE

	Crib/Wall	Twin	Double	Queen	King
Stenciled blocks:					
Light background	1	2½	3	3⅜	4
Dark for corner triangles	¼	¾	1	1	1¼
Pieced blocks:					
Combination one: 2 fabrics, *each*	¼	¼	¼	¼	¼
Combination two: 2 fabrics, *each*	⅜	⅜	⅜	⅜	⅜
Combination three: 2 fabrics, *each*	⅜	⅝	⅝	⅝	⅝
Combination four: 2 fabrics, *each*	¼	⅝	⅝	⅝	⅝
Combination five: 2 fabrics, *each*	—	⅝	⅝	⅞	⅞
Combination six: 2 fabrics, *each*	—	½	⅝	⅝	⅞
Combination seven: 2 fabrics, *each*	—	¼	⅜	½	⅝
Combination eight: 2 fabrics, *each*	—	—	¼	¼	½
Combination nine: 2 fabrics, *each*	—	—	—	—	¼
Border	1½	2⅝	2⅝	2⅝	3
Backing	1½	5½	5½	8¼	9
Binding	½	¾	1	1	1¼

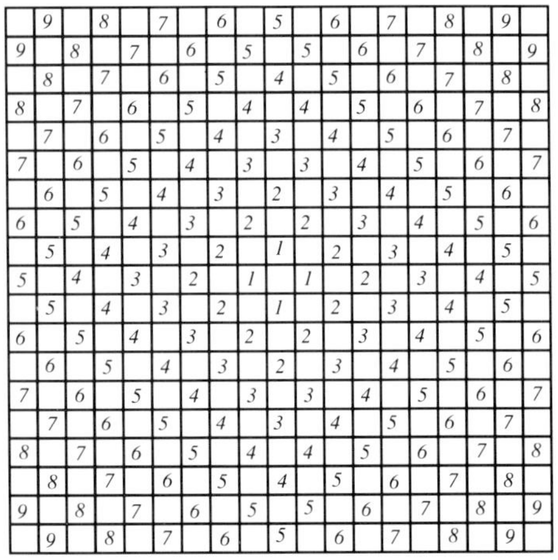

Layout of Blocks

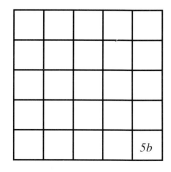

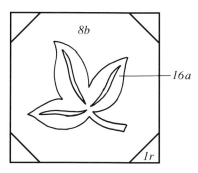

CUTTING

	Crib/Wall	Twin	Double	Queen	King
Stenciled blocks:					
Light:					
Template 8b	32	111	127	145	181
– OR –					
Quick: number of strips	5	16	19	21	26
Dark:					
Template 1r	128	444	508	580	724
– OR –					
Quick: number of strips	5	16	19	21	26
Pieced blocks:					
Template 5b:					
Light	416	1430	1664	1872	2340
Dark	384	1320	1536	1728	2160
– OR –					
Quick:					
Combination one:					
# of light strips	5	5	5	5	5
# of dark strips	5	5	5	5	5
Combination two:					
# of light strips	8	8	8	8	8
# of dark strips	7	7	7	7	7
Combination three:					
# of light strips	8	13	13	13	13
# of dark strips	7	12	12	12	12
Combination four:					
# of light strips	5	13	13	13	13
# of dark strips	5	12	12	12	12
Combination five:					
# of light strips	—	13	13	18	18
# of dark strips	—	12	12	17	17
Combination six:					
# of light strips	—	10	13	13	18
# of dark strips	—	10	12	12	17
Combination seven:					
# of light strips	—	5	8	10	13
# of dark strips	—	5	7	10	12
Combination eight:					
# of light strips	—	—	5	5	10
# of dark strips	—	—	5	5	10
Combination nine:					
# of light strips	—	—	—	—	5
# of dark strips	—	—	—	—	5
Border: width	4½″	4½″	4½″	4½″	4½″
Backing: number of lengths	1	2	2	3	3

Stenciled by Ren Brown and made by Laura Nownes, Katie Prindle and Diana McClun

Step 2

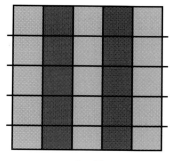

Set #1

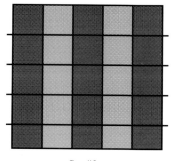

Set #2

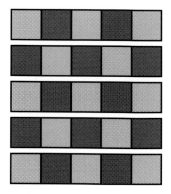

Step 2

Quick cutting:
- For 8b: Cut 5½"-wide strips. Then cut to 5½" squares. You may choose to mark 5½" squares on your full piece of fabric, stencil and then cut all the blocks apart.
- For 1r: Cut 1½"-wide strips. Then cut to 1½" squares.
- For 5b: Cut 1½"-wide strips.

CONSTRUCTION

Stenciled blocks: Use Template 16a.

1. Stencil a leaf design onto each background piece. Detailed instructions for stenciling the leaf are given in the practice exercise for stenciling.

2. For the corner triangles, use Template 1r (traditional) or 1½" squares (quick). If quick methods are used, refer to the instructions for double half-square triangles for help.

Pieced blocks:

Each pieced block requires two sets of strips.

1. Sew your 1½"-wide strips together to make the required number of sets for each combination:

	Crib/Wall	Twin	Double	Queen	King
Combination one:					
Set # 1	1	1	1	1	1
Set # 2	1	1	1	1	1
Combination two:					
Set # 1	2	2	2	2	2
Set # 2	1	1	1	1	1
Combination three:					
Set # 1	2	3	3	3	3
Set # 2	1	2	2	2	2
Combination four:					
Set # 1	1	3	3	3	3
Set # 2	1	2	2	2	2
Combination five:					
Set # 1	—	3	3	4	4
Set # 2	—	2	2	3	3
Combination six:					
Set # 1	—	2	3	3	4
Set # 2	—	2	2	2	3
Combination seven:					
Set # 1	—	1	2	2	3
Set # 2	—	1	1	2	2
Combination eight:					
Set # 1	—	—	1	1	2
Set # 2	—	—	1	1	2
Combination nine:					
Set # 1	—	—	—	—	1
Set # 2	—	—	—	—	1

2. Cut each set of strips apart every 1½". Then sew them together to make each *Twenty-Five Patch* block, exactly as shown in the diagram.

3. Sew the blocks together in a straight set, alternating pieced blocks and stenciled blocks.

CHAPTER 8

MEDALLION QUILTS

SUPPLIES:
Graph paper, ⅛″ grid
Sharp lead pencil
C-Thru plastic 2″ × 18″ ruler (B-85)
Design board
Reducing glass (optional)
Plastic or metal tape measure
Fabric scissors – OR –
Rotary cutter
Glass-head pins
Right-angle triangle – OR –
Ruler with 45-degree angle (for mitered and border-printed borders)
Sewing machine – OR –
Hand sewing needle
Cotton thread
Steam iron
Pressing surface
Light-colored towel

 Until 1850, the stylish and formal medallion quilt was reserved by American and British needlewomen for some of their finest and most elaborate work. And, as we shall demonstrate in the examples we offer here, the medallion quilt is a versatile style, and fun to make.

Some of the most famous and treasured of early American medallion quilts contain at their centers kerchiefs printed by Philadelphian John Hewson who, in 1773, smuggled his printing equipment out of England and brought it—and his extensive knowledge—to the colonies. Others contain appliqué or Broderie Perse, while some are filled with trapunto or are stenciled. Still others contain oversized or multiple pieced blocks, usually set on point to dramatize the pieced patterns.

Here is a quilt style that adapts to pieced work, appliqué or Broderie Perse, trapunto, stenciling and even crazy patchwork. You can use several of these in one quilt, creating a quilt that is simultaneously visually dynamic and orderly.

Medallion quilts look great in any size and are wonderful when displayed on a wall or bed. And here is a quilt style that any beginner can enjoy or that an experienced needleworker can make as challenging as she or he desires.

Create a medallion quilt. It's great fun!

PLANNING YOUR MEDALLION QUILT

There are many components which can be incorporated into your medallion quilt. Consider some of our suggestions, or create your own. Experiment with several different arrangements.

Straight

On Point

Center design: Pieced, appliquéd, trapunto, crazy patchwork or stenciled block or a printed fabric such as a scarf.
- Straight or on point
- Four blocks joined
- Blocks joined with sashing, straight or on point
- Six blocks joined with or without sashing

Borders:
- Plain
- Printed
- Pieced
- Appliquéd
- Trapunto
- Crazy patchwork
- Stenciled

Corner blocks:
- Plain
- Printed
- Pieced
- Appliquéd
- Trapunto
- Crazy patchwork
- Stenciled

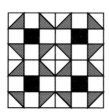

*Four Blocks
Straight Set*

*Four Blocks
On Point*

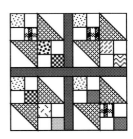

*Blocks with Sashing
Straight Set*

*Blocks with Sashing
On Point*

Six Blocks

*Six Blocks
with Sashing*

CHOOSE A CENTER DESIGN

The focal point of a medallion quilt is the center design. A 15″ or larger block design works well for this style of quilt.

Consider using one of your favorite pieced block patterns, such as *Feathered Star.* With your knowledge of drafting learned in Chapter One, you can make the pieced block in any size, or consider joining four blocks together to form a larger square (or six for a rectangular design).

If appliqué appeals to you, one of our featured appliqué patterns, such as *Rose of Sharon* or *Wedding Rose,* would make a beautiful center design. Any of the wonderful stencil designs available would also be suitable for a center motif. If you enjoy Broderie Perse, you might decide to create your own design from cut-out motifs.

Whichever you choose, it is important that the central motif be a strong, interesting design, able to maintain the focus of attention and not be overpowered by the borders.

SELECT A COLOR SCHEME

Unlike many quilts which repeat fabrics and colors through the individual pattern blocks, the medallion quilt allows for a variety of fabrics and colors. Allow yourself enough different fabric, in both color and design: light, medium, dark; small to large prints; and solids. For optimum experimentation, you will want to have a large fabric palette (about 8 to 10 fabrics) with which to work and play.

As you will discover, much of the color process for a medallion quilt is trial and error, as each new border must not only relate to the central design but also act as a transition from a previous border. Color is a very important factor, and you may find that the 2″ border you have planned works better in a medium than a dark fabric. Having several fabrics to work with will make this process easier. ✷ *Helpful hint:* If choosing a color scheme is difficult for you, consider using a favorite printed fabric or an article from nature (such as a flower) for help. Simply take the fabric or object to your fabric store and use the colors contained in it as a guide when choosing your fabrics.

More details on establishing a color scheme can be found in our own *Quilts! Quilts!! Quilts!!!* and Mary Coyne Penders' wonderful guide to color and fabric selection, *Color and Cloth*.

AVOID PROBLEMS: GRAPH IT!

Medallion quilts can incorporate many different design elements; it is helpful to have a basic idea of what the quilt will look like before investing many hours into making pieced or appliquéd borders, only to discover that they are not what you want. The easiest way to get an overall feel for your finished quilt and to avoid making design mistakes is to plan your quilt on graph paper.

You may cringe at the thought of working on graph paper. This is only because you have not allowed yourself to experiment with it before. It is fun to be the designer of your own quilt. It can be a very rewarding process and also *a great time and grief saver.* Pre-planning on graph paper allows you to experiment with proportion, numbers and size of the borders. It gives you a starting point when working with border measurements. You can play with design elements and see the relationship of the borders to each other and to the center design. As you can imagine, it is much easier to make adjustments on paper than on fabric. You will know in advance how much yardage is required and the size to which each border should be cut.

WORK ON A DESIGN BOARD

Planning your medallion quilt on graph paper is very helpful, but be prepared to make a few adjustments in your final design. When fabric and color come into play, many things can change. What looks great on paper will not necessarily translate perfectly into the real world of fabrics and colors. You may have to make an adjustment in border width or pieced design so that the overall quilt will maintain balance. We suggest working with your quilt on a design board (a wall or board covered with flannel or pellon fleece) and viewing it through a reducing glass.

Begin by placing your center design onto the design board. Experiment with different printed border fabrics. Rather than cutting strips of many border fabrics, simply fold a particular fabric several times lengthwise and place it along one side of the center block. This will avoid wasted fabric. For pieced border strips, you can make a few pieced blocks or simply cut some shapes from different fabrics. Then you can experiment with many combinations. Remember, this is easily done, since the fabric sticks to your design board.

A few things to keep in mind when translating the design from paper to fabric:

1. Dark colors will add weight. They will work well for narrow borders to frame and separate designs.

2. Light colors are airy and work well for background.

3. Dull colors will appear to recede.

4. Bright colors will stand out and attract attention.

PLAN YOUR BORDERS

You want your borders to complement and not overpower the center design. Your borders will separate the design elements as well as increase the size of the quilt to fit a particular bed or wall size. Some suggested borders are:

1. *Plain:* Borders of any width made from solid fabric. They can provide a space where quilting or trapunto designs can be used to add texture.

2. *Printed:* Borders of any width made from printed fabric. The print itself can give texture to the quilt rather than being dependent upon the quilting stitches. Printed borders are useful because the quilting stitches can often follow the design or print of the pattern, thereby avoiding any marking. Fabric which is printed with lengthwise design (called border-printed fabric) is an easy way of adding texture and color to your quilt.

3. *Multiple:* This is a series of bands, plain, printed or a combination of the two. These borders are used to enlarge the quilt with more than one color or texture. They provide an opportunity for repetition of a color or colors which may have been used in the center motif. They also allow for varied border widths which add visual interest to your quilt.

4. *Pieced:* This type of border provides an opportunity to repeat a block design (or elements of a block design) which may have been used in the center motif. It allows you to add pieced work to a medallion quilt

with an appliquéd, stenciled, trapunto or crazy patchwork center. You can even have a pieced center with different pieced patterns in your borders (such as a quilt with a *Feathered Star* center and *Le Moyne Star*s in some of its borders).

5. *Appliquéd:* Appliquéd flowers, vines, leaves, swags and curved stems can modify the linearity of your quilt. Appliquéd borders can also complement your central motif by repeating or varying some of its elements.

6. *Stenciled:* This type of border is a quick and easy way of achieving some of the same effects as an appliquéd border.

CONSTRUCTING YOUR MEDALLION QUILT

If you have taken the time to pre-plan your quilt on graph paper, you will know the cut size and finished size of each border strip. *Unless you are very confident about the final placement of your fabrics,* we recommend that you cut each border fabric as needed rather than cutting all fabrics at the outset. You will want to experiment with several fabrics, and cutting too soon can sometimes result in wasted pieces.

Cut your border strips, allowing enough length for the type of corner treatment you would like to use, either straight or mitered. Straight borders are appropriate for plain, pieced, multiple, stenciled, appliquéd and printed (not border-printed) borders. Mitered borders are especially attractive with border-printed fabric and are appropriate for all borders except most pieced ones, as the seams joining the pieced units may interfere with the seam required to miter the corner.

Start with an accurately measured and cut center block. You will be fitting the center block to the first row of border strips *rather than* the border strips to the center block. Each subsequent border must be pre-measured, cut and marked before being sewn to the previously attached borders. If you simply cut strips and sew them without first marking the desired finished length, you will almost always end up with rippled edges, as the strips will stretch during sewing.

Nothing is more frustrating than investing the time and work into making a beautiful medallion quilt, only to have the edges ripple with the addition of each new border. This can be avoided with careful measuring, pressing and sewing techniques. We call this "squaring up your quilt," which means that corners must be 90-degree angles and opposite sides of the same measurement. *Your quilt top must be squared up after the addition of each new border strip.* If not, the problems will compound.

You can make a successful medallion quilt, if you will take the time to read through and follow these few but important instructions.

MEASURING

To determine the required length for border strips, lay the center block (quilt top) out on a flat, rigid surface and use a plastic or metal tape

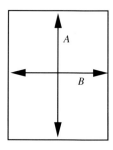

Measuring

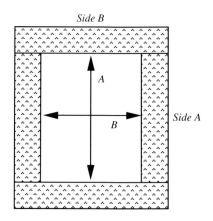

Side B

Side A

Step 5

measure to determine Dimension A (the longer dimension) and Dimension B (the shorter dimension) of your center block across its center. This center measurement is more accurate, as the edges of the center motif may be stretched, causing opposite sides to differ.

With the exception of pieced borders, it is advisable to cut your border strips longer than needed. The type of corner treatment desired (straight or mitered) will determine the additional length required. After the border is sewn to the quilt top and pressed, you can square up the corners and trim off any excess length. It is important to take time to measure the quilt top before you add each new border. Cut the border strips and mark them borders A or B. If you will take time to measure, mark, sew, press and cut accurately as described below, you will prevent the edges of the borders from rippling.

ATTACHING STRAIGHT BORDERS

1. Once you have measured and cut your A and B border strips, place pins at the center points of the two A border strips. Measure out from the pins in each direction a distance equal to one-half the A dimension. Place pins at these points to mark the corners.

2. Place pins at the center points along sides A of the quilt top.

3. Lay these border strips on each A side of the quilt top, right sides together, matching pins with corners and at the center points.

4. Sew the border strips to the quilt top. Ease in any fullness if necessary.

5. Press the border strips flat. Then trim the excess length of border fabric even with the B sides of the quilt top.

6. Determine the new B dimension (which includes the width of the A border strips).

7. Mark the two remaining border strips and the B sides of the quilt top, with pins at their center points. Measure out from the pins in each direction on the border strips, a distance equal to one-half *the new B dimension*. Place pins at these points to mark the corners.

8. Attach these border strips to the quilt top, using the same method described in Steps 3 and 4 above.

9. Press the border strips flat. Then trim the excess length of border fabric even with the A sides of the quilt top.

ATTACHING MITERED BORDERS

Two or more non-pieced borders can be sewn together and treated as one border. Match the center points of the border strips to each other. Sew them together lengthwise in one unit before sewing to the quilt top. Treat this unit now as one border strip and use the technique described below. ◨ *Warning:* These strips must be joined evenly and pressed carefully in order to avoid misshapen edges.

1. Place pins at the center points of the two A border strips. Measure out from the pins in each direction a distance equal to one-half the A dimension. Place pins at these points to mark the corners.

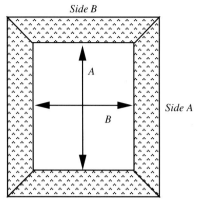
Mitered Borders

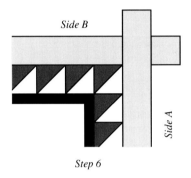
Step 6

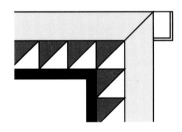
Step 7

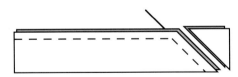
Step 11

2. Place pins at the center points along sides A of the quilt top.

3. Lay these border strips on each A side of the quilt top, right sides together, matching pins with corners and at the center points.

4. Sew the borders to the quilt top, beginning and ending *1/4" from each corner.* Ease in any fullness if necessary.

5. Using the same method, sew the B borders to the B sides of the quilt.

6. Take the quilt to the pressing surface. Working on one corner of the quilt at a time, extend the unsewn border ends out straight, overlapping the end of A over the end of B.

7. Lift up the A border strip and fold it under *only itself,* at a 45-degree angle. The remainder of border A should lie even with both sides of the underlying B border.

8. Using your right-angle triangle or ruler with a 45-degree angle, check to see that the angle is accurate and the corner is square. Place pins to hold the border strips in place. Then press to set the angle.

9. Turn the quilt top to the wrong side and place pins near the pressed fold in the corner to hold the border strips in place.

10. Take the quilt top to the sewing machine and, with the wrong side facing up, stitch along the folded line in the corner.

11. Trim all excess fabric from the border strips.

12. Repeat for the remaining three corners.

ATTACHING BORDERS OF BORDER-PRINTED FABRIC

When using border-printed fabric, it is important that the corners be the same, or at least that opposite corners match. Be sure to purchase extra fabric for matching. These borders look best when the corners are mitered. However, look at the Broderie Perse medallion quilt on page 161. In keeping with the tradition of nineteenth-century medallion quilts, Bernice Stone did not miter the corners of the border-printed fabric. If you are making a square medallion quilt, you will not have any difficulty in getting the designs to match in the corners, as long as you place a similar design at the center point of each side. A rectangular medallion quilt is a little more challenging:

1. Use a metal or plastic tape measure to determine the A and B dimensions of the quilt top across the center. Write these figures down.

2. Place pins at the center points of each side of the quilt top.

3. You will be fitting the quilt top to the border strips *rather than* the border strips to the quilt top. This will prevent the edges of the borders from rippling. Choose a design in your border-printed fabric to be positioned at the center points of sides A of your quilt top. Mark it with pins. Measure out from the pins in each direction a distance equal to one-half the A dimension. Place pins at these points to mark the corners. Do the same on the other A border strip.

4. Lay one of these borders strips on each A side of the quilt top, right sides together, matching pins with corners and at the center points. Use more pins to attach the borders in place. Beginning and ending 1/4" from

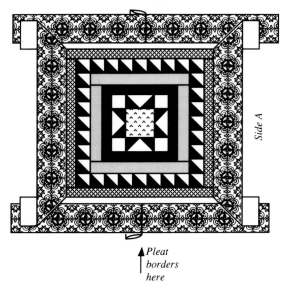

Side B

Side A

▲*Pleat*
borders
here

Border Printed Fabric

each corner, stitch the A borders to the quilt, with the border strips on top. There will be a generous amount of fabric from both ends of the borders extending beyond the quilt top. This is needed to miter the corners. *Do not cut it off.*

5. Take the quilt top to the pressing surface and fold all four unsewn extensions of the borders back to form 45-degree angles. Check the accuracy of the angles with a ruler marked with a 45-degree angle. Press a fold in the angles.

6. Take the quilt top to a flat surface. Lay a B border strip along a B side of the quilt top. Line up the same design in the border fabric chosen in Step 3 above with the center point of side B. The excess B border strip lengths must extend *under* the folded corners of the previously attached A border strips.

7. Pull the B border strip together at its center, forming a pleat. Watch the designs forming in the corners and continue pulling until you find one you like. Make sure you are pulling equal amounts from each end so that the corner designs will match each other. Now fold the pleat to the wrong side of the border strip and pin.

8. Repeat for the other B side of the quilt top.

9. Place pins in the corners to hold the joining of the A and B borders in place.

10. Turn each B border strip right side down on the quilt top. Place pins along the edge to attach it to the quilt top, pinning from the corners to the center pleat.

11. Fold the quilt top in half lengthwise, right side out. The pleats will extend beyond the center folds in the quilt top.

12. Stitch along each pleat even with the fold in the quilt top. Trim the excess to within 1/4" of the stitching line. Press the seams in each B border strip to one side.

13. Unfold the quilt top and stitch your B border strips to it, beginning and ending 1/4" from each corner.

14. To miter the corners, stitch along the folds which were pressed into the A border strips. For more details see Steps 9–11 in "Attaching Mitered Borders."

15. Press on the right side.

ATTACHING PIECED BORDERS

This type of border often presents a problem for quilters. The question always is: what size should the individual pieced units be to fit evenly onto each side of the quilt? The key word here is "evenly." It would be ideal if each pieced border could in fact fit evenly, but this is not always the case. We do our best to make the border strip the right size and then, with a little adjustment, make it work.

1. Find the A and B measurements of the quilt as described in "Measuring." Write these figures down on a piece of paper.

2. This step involves playing around with figures. Determine in your mind the approximate size you would like the pieced units to be—for example, 1½" squares, 2" half-square triangles, 4" pieced blocks, etc. Then divide the measurement into the figures determined in Step 1. Does it divide evenly into both measurements, or is the result a fraction for one or both figures? If it divides evenly, then you are one of the lucky few. Take, for example, a quilt which measures 48"×64". You would like to add a 2" sawtooth border of half-square triangle units around each side. 2" divides evenly into both 48" and 64". You would need to make 24 units for each A side and 32 units for each B side, plus four additional units for the corners.

That was relatively easy, but quiltmaking does not always work out this neatly. More often than not, you will end up with a situation where the quilt top measures 47"×64". Again, you want to add a 2" sawtooth border of half-square triangle units. 2" does not divide evenly into 47": the result is 23½. Obviously you can't make a half unit, so you will round up to the next whole number and make 24 units for each of the B sides. You will take a slightly larger seam allowance when joining a few units together to take up the additional 1/2". Spread the adjusting measurement (in this case, 1/2") out over the length of the pieced strip and it will never be noticed.

3. Sew the two A border strips to the A sides of the quilt top.

4. Attach a corner unit to each end of the B border strips. Then sew these border strips to the B sides of the quilt top.

If you carefully plan your quilt top on graph paper, you can probably avoid having to adjust the lengths of your pieced borders drastically. But, be prepared for some adjusting nevertheless.

STENCILED MEDALLION

Stenciled by Ren Brown and pieced by Laura Nownes

Center block: 15″

Finished size: 47″ × 47″. (NOTE: A larger quilt can be made by simply adding more borders.)

Techniques: Stenciling, quick cutting, half-square triangles and double half-square triangles or Templates 1n, 3b, 4k and 5g

Fabric suggestions: Light background and nine fabrics for pieced and printed borders

YARDAGE

Light for background	2⅛
Medium for zig zag border	¼
Dark for zig zag border	¼
Dark for narrow borders and binding	⅜
Medium for printed and sawtooth borders	¾
Medium blue	1¼
Wild Goose Chase border, four fabrics, *each*	¼
Backing	3

CUTTING

Cut all your fabrics crossgrain unless indicated otherwise.

Background fabric:

Center block: number of 15½" squares	1
Stenciled border: number of 4"-wide strips	4
Template 4k	36
– OR –	
Quick: number of 3½"-wide strips	2
Template 3b	308
– OR –	
Quick: number of 2"-wide strips	11
and number of 2⅜"-wide strips	3
Template 5g	4
– OR –	
Quick: number of 2"-wide strips	1

Medium (for zig zag border):

Template 1n reverse	24
– OR –	
Quick: number of 2"-wide strips	2
and number of 2⅜"-wide strips	1

Dark (for zig zag border):

Template 1n	24
– OR –	
Quick: number of 2"-wide strips	2
and number of 2⅜"-wide strips	1

Dark (for narrow borders):

Number of ¾"-wide strips	8
Number of 1"-wide strips	4

Medium (for printed and sawtooth borders):

Number of 1½"-wide strips	4
Template 3b	68
– OR –	
Quick: number of 2⅜"-wide strips	2

Medium (for printed border): Cut lengthwise

Number of 1½"-wide strips	12

***Wild Goose Chase* fabrics:**

Template 4k	112
– OR –	
Quick: number of 3½"-wide strips of *each* fabric	2
Backing: number of lengths	2

Quick cutting
- For 1n and 1n reversed: Cut the 2″-wide strips to 2″ squares.

    Cut the 2⅜″-wide strips to 2⅜″ squares. Then cut each square in *half diagonally*.
- For 4k: Cut the 3½″-wide strips to 2″ × 3½″ rectangles.
- For 3b: Cut the 2″-wide strips to 2″ squares.

    Cut the 2⅜″-wide strips to 2⅜″ squares. Then cut each square in *half diagonally*.
- For 5g: Cut the 2″-wide strips to 2″ squares.

STENCILING

Use Templates 19a and 20a. For detailed instruction on stenciling fabric, read Chapter Seven (Stenciled Quilts).

1. Using an ultra-fine permanent pen, trace the pattern onto a piece of tracing paper. Label the individual shapes 1, 2 or 3. Be sure to include the dotted center registration marks and corners.

2. There are three stencils required for this pattern (see templates). Using an ultra-fine permanent pen, trace all of the number 1 shapes onto a piece of mylar, coming in at least 1/2″ from the edges of the mylar. Trace all of the number 2 shapes and then number 3 shapes onto two separate pieces of mylar. Be sure to include center and corner registration marks on all stencils. ✷ *Helpful hint:* All three stencils can be traced onto a 19″ × 23″ piece of mylar. Then, using an X-Acto knife and glass cutting surface, cut the shapes from the mylar.

3. Lay your 15½″ square of background fabric onto a piece of cardboard or heavy paper. Center stencil 1 over the fabric, lining up the corner registration marks with the corners and right-hand cut edge of the fabric. Tape in place.

4. Apply paint to all the shapes contained in stencil 1.

5. Allow the paint to dry on the stencil before turning it over and taping it to the other half of the fabric. Be certain to align registration marks. Apply paint to all the shapes.

6. Repeat Steps 3 through 5 for stencil 2, and then stencil 3, using the stencil registration dots for ease in accurately overlaying the stencils.

7. The border design is contained in the lower portion (below the dotted lines) of stencils 1, 2 and 3. Beginning about 4″ in from the left side of one of the border strips, stencil four designs onto two of the 4″-wide border strips. Stencil five designs onto the remaining two 4″-wide border strips (see photograph of quilt). Use the dotted registration marks for determining the distance between each pair of designs. The dotted lines on the stencils should be lined up with the raw edge of the fabric strips.

8. Allow the paint to dry at least 15 minutes. Then heat set, following the instructions given in Chapter Seven.

CONSTRUCTION

Instructions and diagrams are given for both quick and traditional methods of piecing.

Quick Piecing:
Zig zag border:

1. Using the 2″ × 3½″ rectangles of background fabric and the 2″ squares of the medium and dark fabrics, use the double half-square triangle method demonstrated on pages 40–41 to make 36 units:

2. Use the 2⅜″ triangles to make:

8 units:

8 units:

4 units:

3. Make four sets (five units each). Press seams joining the units *open*.

4. Make four sets (six units each):

5. Join sets together to make four.
Press seams *open*. Checkpoint: Each strip should measure 3½″ × 15½″.

6. Make four corner sets:

Sawtooth border:
  1. Use the 2⅜″ triangles to make 68 units:
  2. Make four sets (eight units each):

and make four sets (eight units each):

3. Join sets together to make four new sets:
Checkpoint: Each strip should measure 2″ × 24½″.

Note: The four remaining units are for the corners.

Wild Goose Chase border:
  1. Using the 2″ squares of background fabric and the 2″ × 3½″ rectangles from the *Wild Goose Chase* fabrics, use the double half-square triangle method to make:

Fabric 1: 32 units
Fabrics 2, 3 and 4: 24 units *each*
Fabric 5 (same fabric as used for the dark narrow borders): 8 units

2. Make eight sets (13 units each):

3. Join pairs to make four new sets:
Checkpoint: Each strip should measure 3½″ × 39½″.

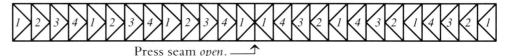

Press seam *open.* ⟶

4. Make four corner sets using the eight Fabric 5 units:

Press seam *open.* ⟶

Traditional Piecing:
Zig zag border: Use Y-seam construction.
   1. Make 20 units:
   Start and stop 1/4″ from each end.
   2. Inset Template 4k.

   3. Make four sets (five units each). Then attach corner and bottom triangles.

   4. Make four corner units:
   5. Inset Template 5g and attach triangles (Template 3b).

Sawtooth border:
   1. Use Template 3b to make 68 units.
   2. Proceed as instructed in "Quick Piecing" above.

Wild Goose Chase border:
   1. Use Templates 4k and 3b to make:

      Fabric 1: 32 units
      Fabrics 2, 3 and 4: 24 units *each*
      Fabric 5 (same fabric as used for dark narrow border): 8 units
   2. Proceed as instructed in "Quick Piecing."

ASSEMBLY

1. Sew two zig zag border strips to two opposite sides of the center block. Attach the corner sets to each end of the remaining strips. Sew them to the two remaining sides of the center block.

2. Attach the 1″-wide strips of dark fabric. Mark two strips at 21½″ for sides A and two strips at 22½″ for sides B.

3. Attach the 1½″-wide strips of sawtooth border fabric. Mark two strips at 22½″ for sides A and two strips at 24½″ for sides B.

4. Sew two pieced sawtooth border strips to two opposite sides of the quilt top. Sew one of the half-square triangle units to each end of the remaining pieced border strips. Sew them to the quilt top.

5. Attach 1½"-wide strips of the medium printed fabric (shown as blue in the sample). Mark two strips 27½" for sides A and two strips 29½" for sides B.

6. Attach 3/4"-wide strips of dark fabric. Mark two strips at 29½" for sides A and two strips at 30" for sides B.

7. Attach the stenciled borders, paying attention to the direction of the design. Mark two strips at 30" for sides A and two strips at 37" for sides B.

8. Attach 3/4"-wide strips of dark fabric. Mark two strips at 37" for sides A and two strips at 37½" for sides B.

9. Attach 1½"-wide strips of the medium printed fabric. Mark two strips at 37½" for sides A and two strips at 39½" for sides B.

10. Sew two pieced *Wild Goose Chase* border strips to two opposite sides of the quilt top. Sew one corner set to each end of the remaining pieced border strips. Sew them to the quilt top.

11. Attach 1½"-wide strips of the medium printed fabric. Mark two strips at 45½" for sides A and two strips at 47½" for sides B.

12. Your quilt top is now complete and ready for layering, basting, quilting and binding.

BRODERIE PERSE MEDALLION

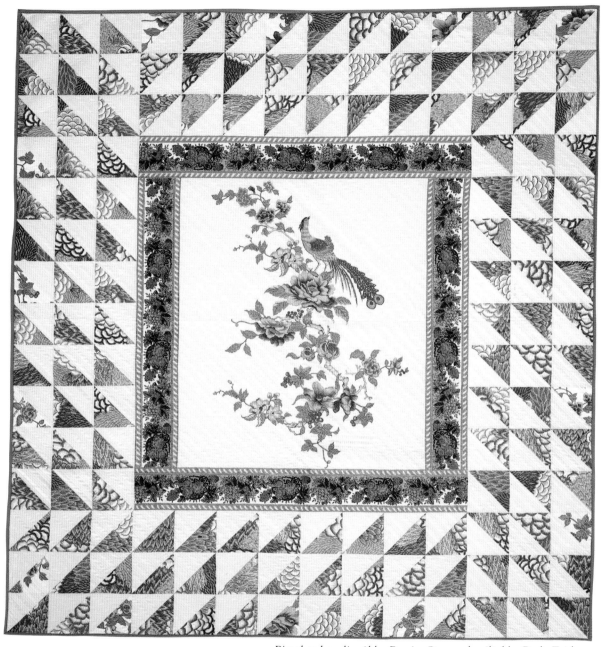

Pieced and appliquéd by Bernice Stone and quilted by Paula Erickson

Techniques: Broderie Perse appliqué and quick cutting or Templates 3m, 3l or 3k

Fabric suggestions: Light background, chintz or Broderie Perse fabric and print fabric for sawtooth border.

NOTE: The width of your border-printed fabric may differ slightly from the suggested widths given below. You can either reduce a strip width or consider using multiple strips. The width is important in order that the sawtooth borders fit evenly. If changes are necessary plan the quilt on graph paper before cutting any fabric to determine exact sizes.

	Crib/Wall	Twin	Double/Queen	King
Finished size	48″×48″	70″×90″	84″×90″	102″×96″

YARDAGE

	Crib/Wall	Twin	Double/Queen	King
Light background	1½	3½	3½	4½
Design fabric*	¾	1½	2	2
Border-printed (or striped) fabric:				
44″-wide fabric	¾	1½	1½	1½
− OR −				
narrow border fabric	2½ at 4½″ wide	5¼ at 5½″ wide	5¼ at 6¾″ wide	5¼ at 6¾″ wide
Print for sawtooth borders	1	2⅛	2½	3½
Backing	3	5½	5½	8½
Binding	½	⅝	1	1

*This is an approximate amount. The repeat of the design will determine the yardage required.

CUTTING

	Crib/Wall	Twin	Double/Queen	King
Light background:				
Center block	16½″ × 16½″	30½″ × 50½″	36″ × 42″	36″ × 42″
Light background and sawtooth border print, *each*				
Template 3m	99	—	—	—
− OR −				
Quick: number of strips*	7	—	—	—
Template 3l	—	156	—	—
− OR −				
Quick: number of strips*	—	12	—	—
Template 3k	—	—	138	200
− OR −				
Quick: number of strips*	—	—	12	17
Border-printed fabric†				
Two for sides A at:	4½″ × 16½″	5½″ × 50½″	6¾″ × 42″	6¾″ × 42″
Two for sides B at:	4½″ × 24½″	5½″ × 40½″	6¾″ × 48½″	6¾″ × 48½″
Backing: number of lengths	1	2	2	3

*Or use grid method for half-square triangles.
†In keeping with the tradition of the nineteenth-century medallion quilts, the corners of the border-printed fabric are not mitered.

Quick cutting: Cut all fabrics crossgrain.
- For 3m: Cut 4⅞″-wide strips. Then cut to 4⅞″ squares. Cut each square in *half diagonally.*
- For 3l: Cut 5⅞″-wide strips. Then cut to 5⅞″ squares. Cut each square in *half diagonally.*
- For 3k: Cut 6⅞″-wide strips. Then cut to 6⅞″ squares. Cut each square in *half diagonally.*

CONSTRUCTION

1. Cut out motifs from design fabric.
2. Lay the center block of background fabric on a smooth, flat surface.
3. Arrange the motifs onto the background fabric in a pleasing arrangement. NOTE: A king-size quilt is wider than it is long. Arrange the motifs accordingly.
4. Pin and then heavily baste the motifs to hold them flat.
5. Using either the needle turn or buttonhole stitch method, appliqué the motifs to the background fabric.
6. Attach the border-printed fabric borders, sewing the A strips to the A sides and B strips to the B sides.
7. For sawtooth borders: Sew each triangle from background fabric to a triangle from printed fabric.
8. Sawtooth borders: Sew order (see diagram). NOTE: The king-size quilt has four rows of sawtooth borders. All other sizes have three rows.

CLASS OUTLINE

For the Stenciled Medallion Quilt (shown on page 155)

SUPPLIES:

Background fabric for center block
Consider having the instructor provide each student with a stencil kit for a nominal fee; otherwise, students will be required to bring:
Piece of cardboard (at least 16″ × 16″)
2 or 3 stencil brushes (½″ – ¾″)
Plastic spoons
Paper plate
Masking tape
4 or 5 small jars with lids
X-Acto knife
Black ultra-fine permanent pen
Glass cutting surface
Tracing paper
19″ × 24″ sheet of mylar
Cellophane tape

Four or five 3-hour classes. This class can easily be adapted for an appliqué center and borders, and is appropriate for all levels of experience.

CLASS ONE: STENCILING

Preparation at home: Background fabric: pre-wash (no detergent) and cut one 15½″ square.
In class: Demonstration: tracing pattern, marking and cutting stencils, mixing and applying paint. Students will make stencils and begin stenciling the center block.
Homework: Finish stenciling center block, if necessary.

CLASS TWO: STENCILING

Preparation at home: Pre-wash border strips fabric (no detergent) and cut strips.
In class: Stencil the border strips.
Homework: Complete stenciling the border strips if necessary. Cut all fabrics for pieced borders. This is a large homework assignment; prepare your students for it.

CLASS THREE: PIECED BORDERS

In class: Construct zig zag, sawtooth and *Wild Goose Chase* borders.
Homework: Complete any unfinished pieced borders and cut all straight borders. This is a large homework assignment; prepare your students for it.

CLASS FOUR: ATTACHING BORDERS

In class: Measuring, marking and attaching borders.

Although Class Five is optional, we feel that the students enjoy going home with a nearly completed project. We encourage them to form their own quilting group, meeting together a few times between Class Five and the reunion.

CLASS FIVE: LAYERING AND BASTING

Preparation at home: Prepare backing fabric, including pre-washing (no detergent).
In class: Layer and baste quilts.

REUNION

In approximately six weeks the students meet with us to share their quilts. A binding demonstration is given at this time. We strongly urge that teachers go this extra step for their students. Student enthusiasm, as they share their finished quilts, is catching; if some students were beginners, the chances are they will have been transformed into quiltmakers.

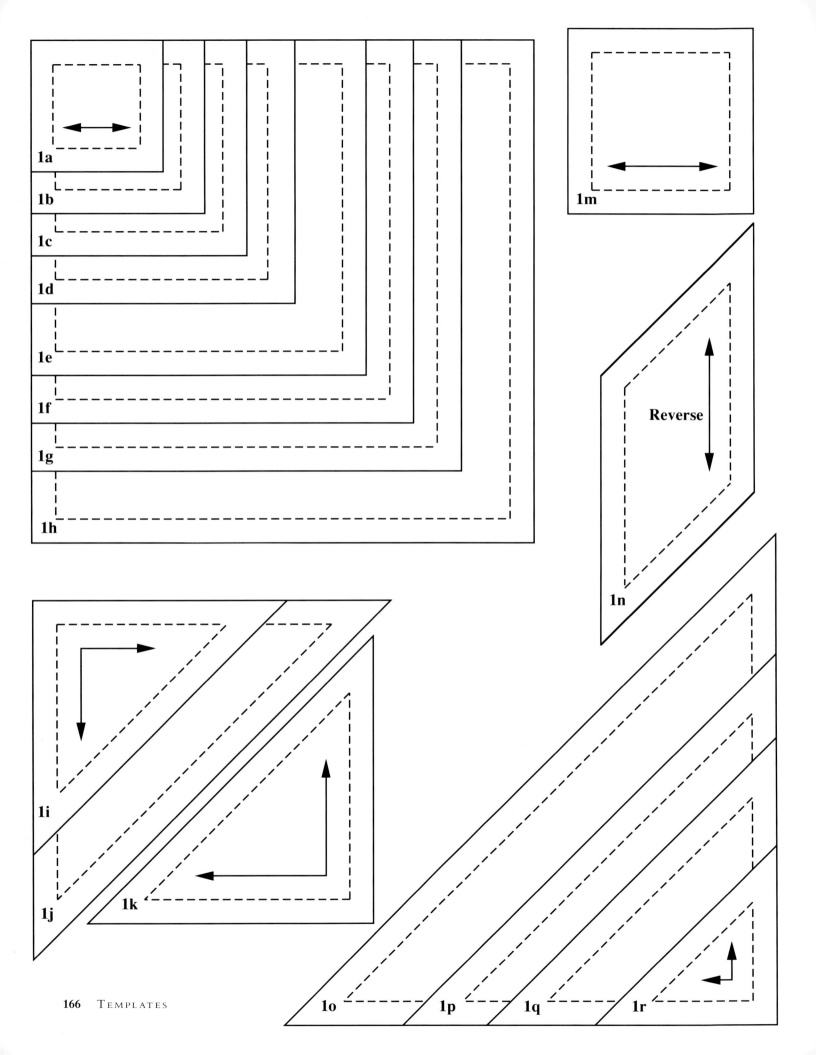

1a

1b

1c

1d

1e

1f

1g

1h

1m

Reverse

1n

1i

1j

1k

1o   1p   1q   1r

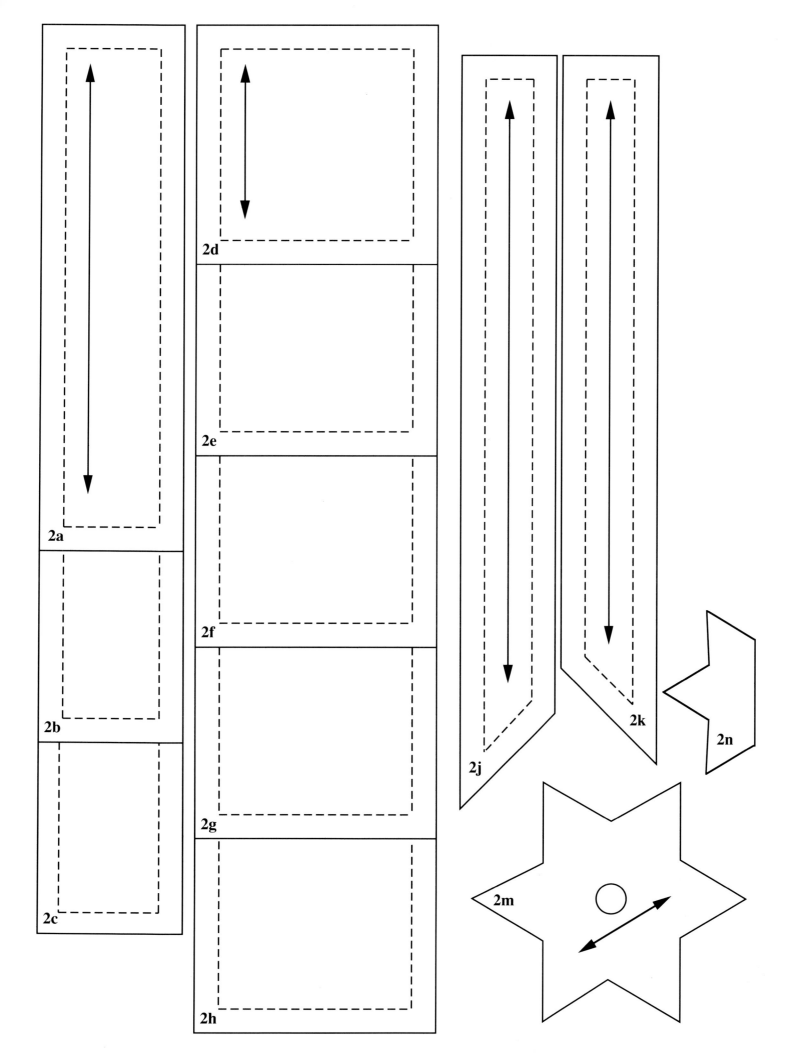

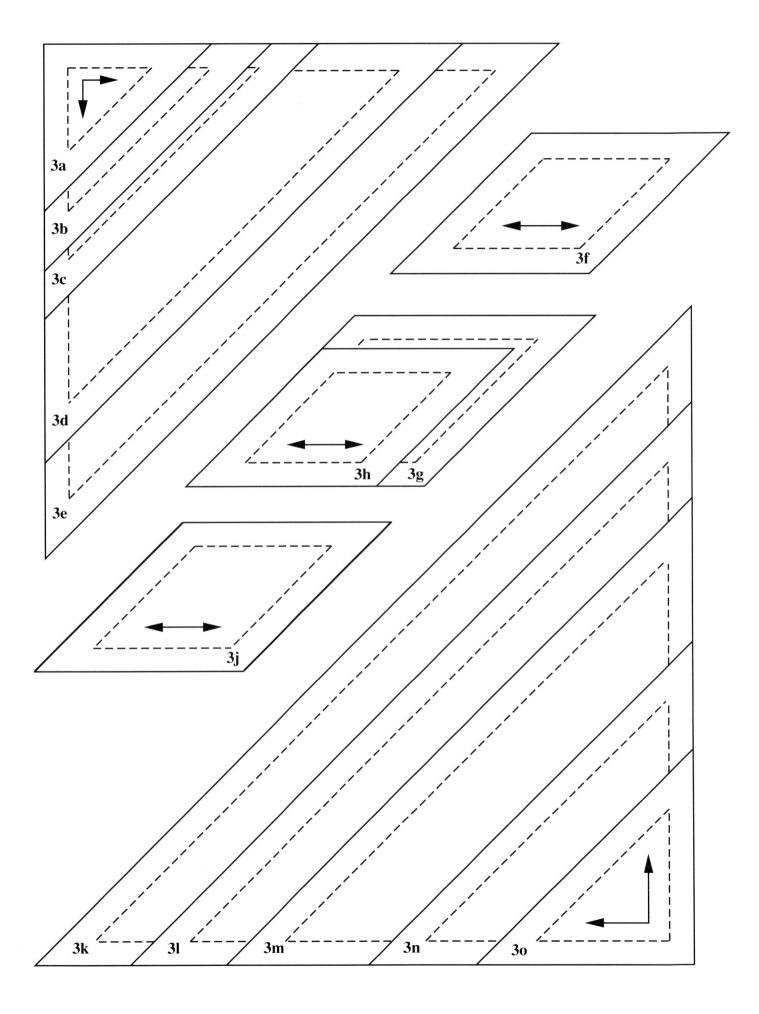

3a

3b

3c

3d

3e

3f

3h   3g

3j

3k   3l   3m   3n   3o

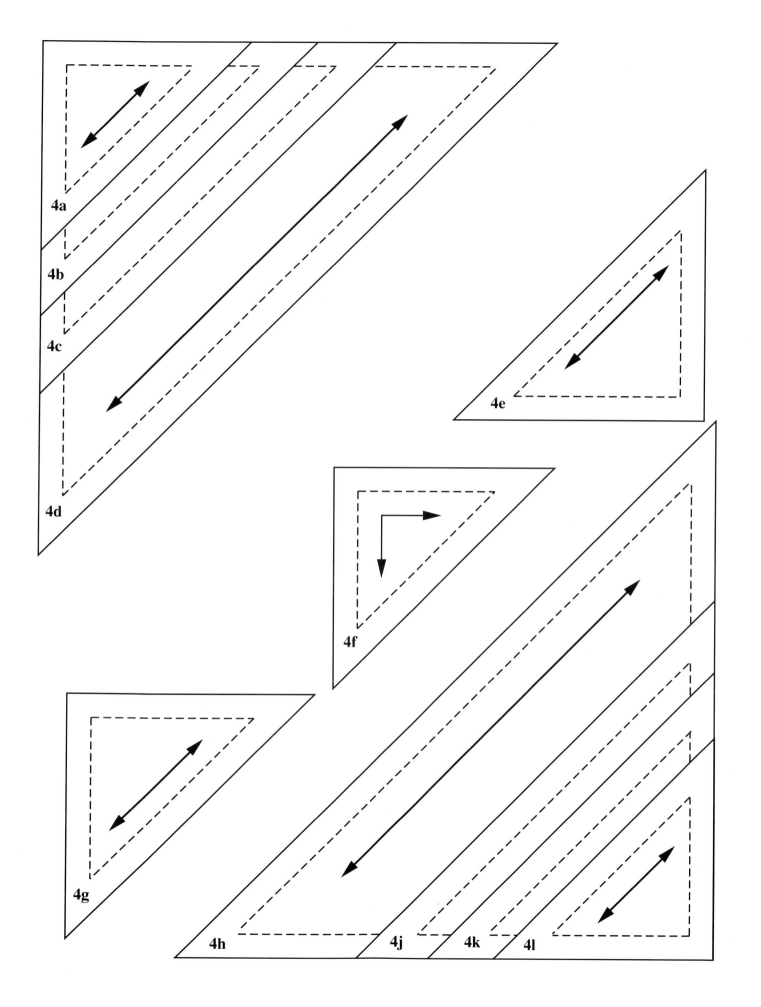

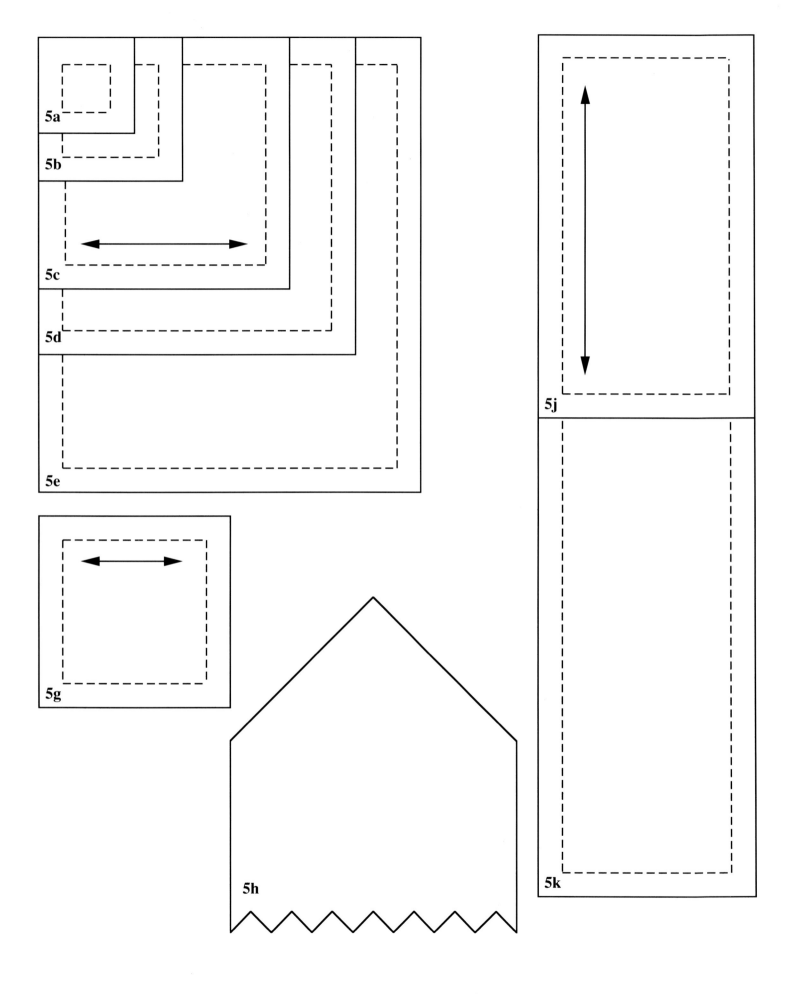

5a

5b

5c

5d

5e

5g

5h

5j

5k

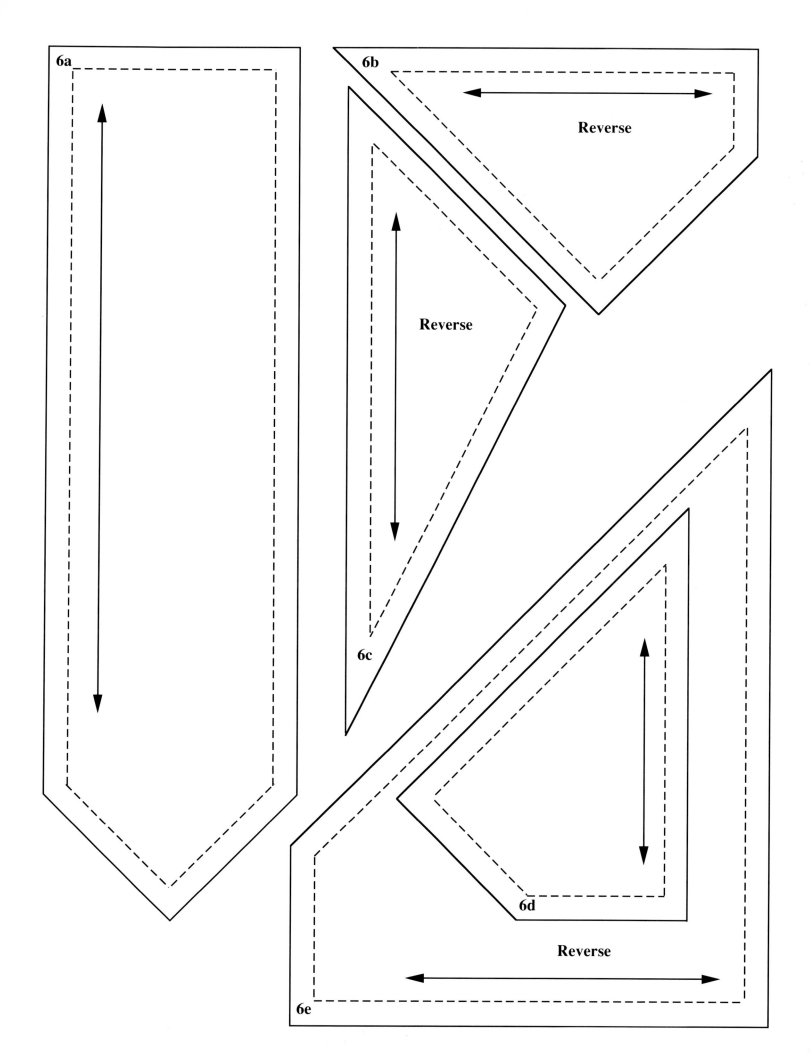

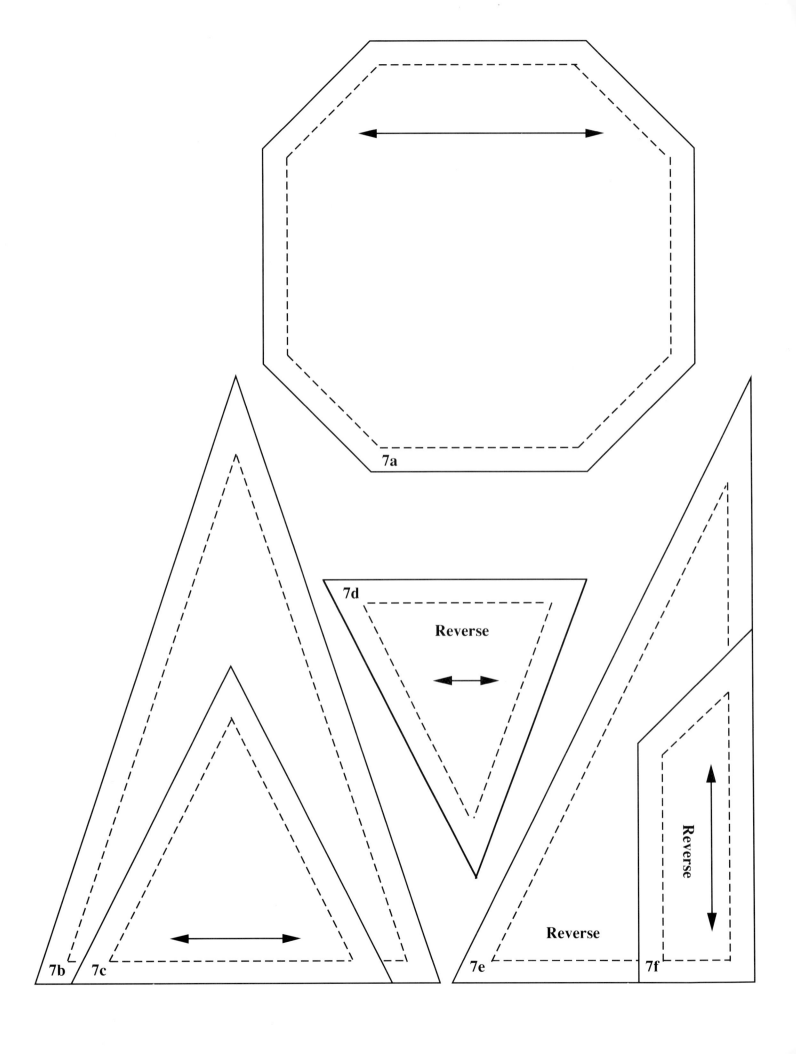

7a

7d

Reverse

7b 7c

Reverse

Reverse

7e 7f

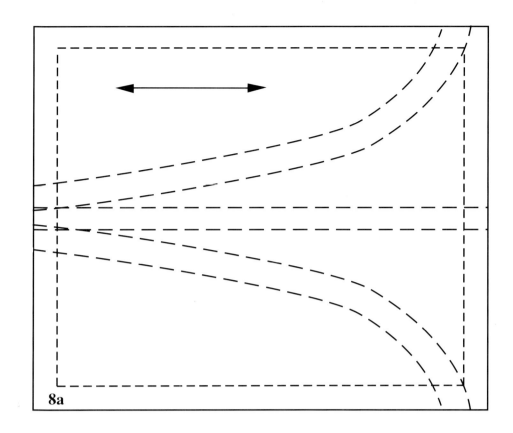

8a

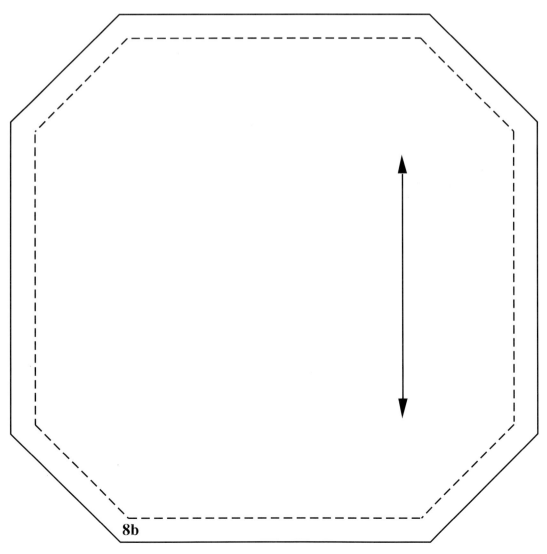

8b

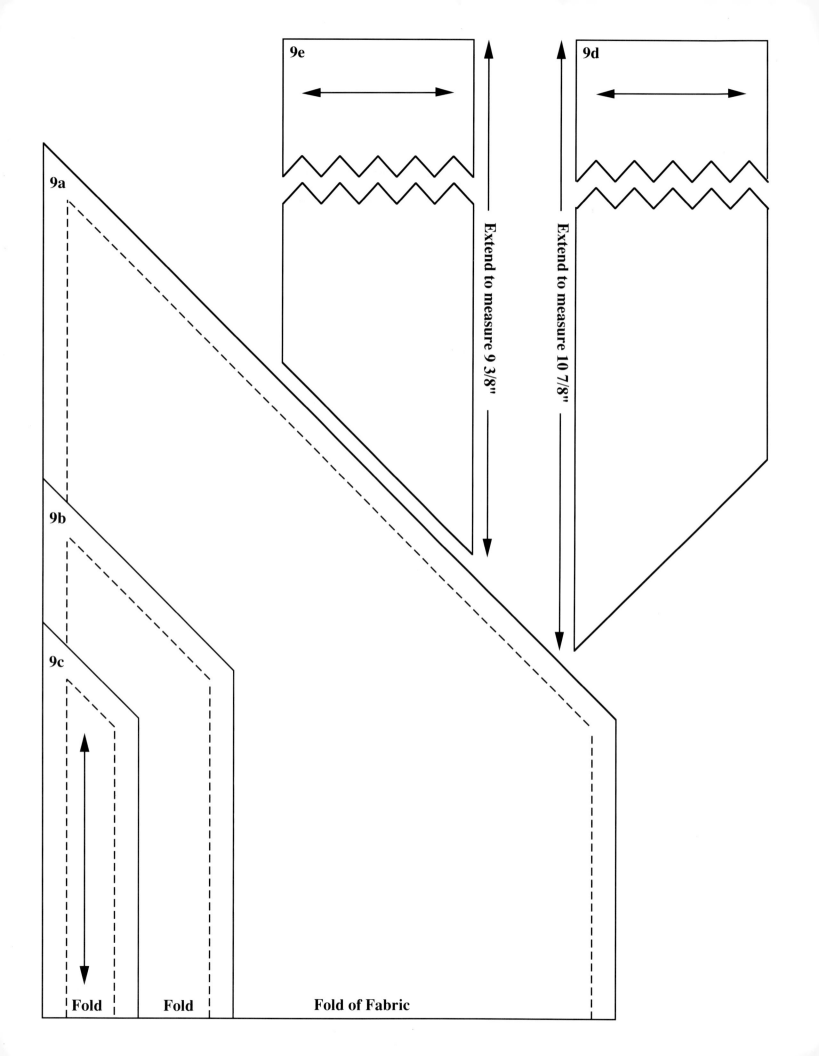

9e

9d

9a

9b

9c

Extend to measure 9 3/8"

Extend to measure 10 7/8"

Fold

Fold

Fold of Fabric

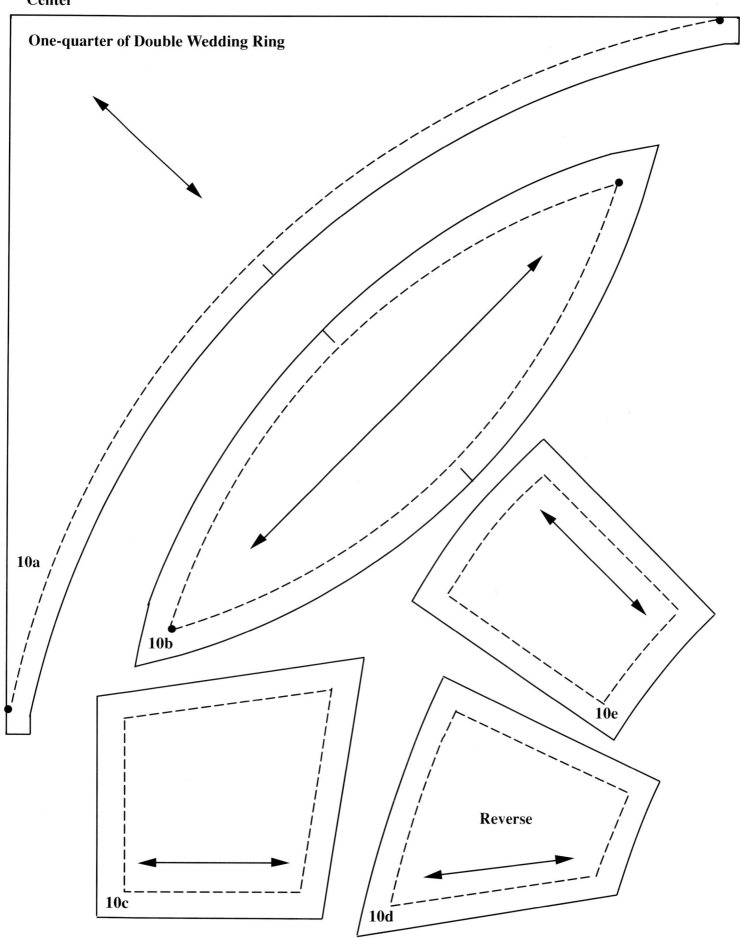

Center

One-quarter of Double Wedding Ring

10a

10b

10c

10d

Reverse

10e

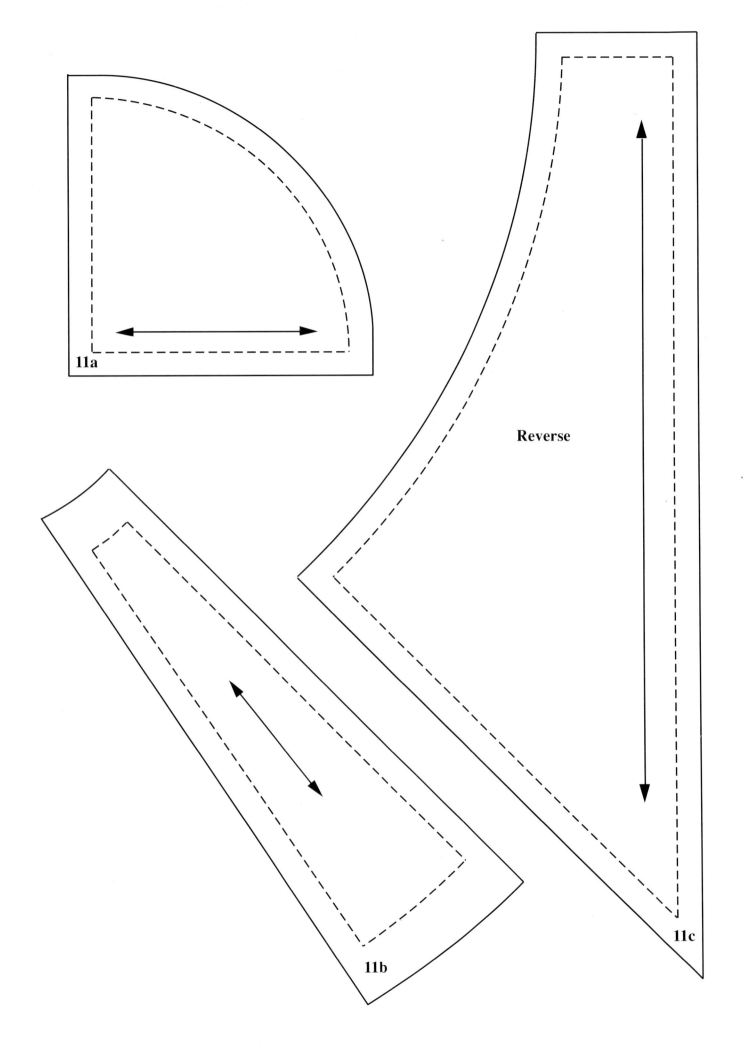

11a

11b

11c

Reverse

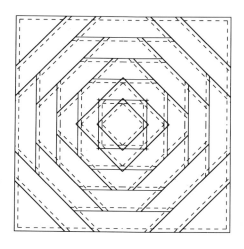

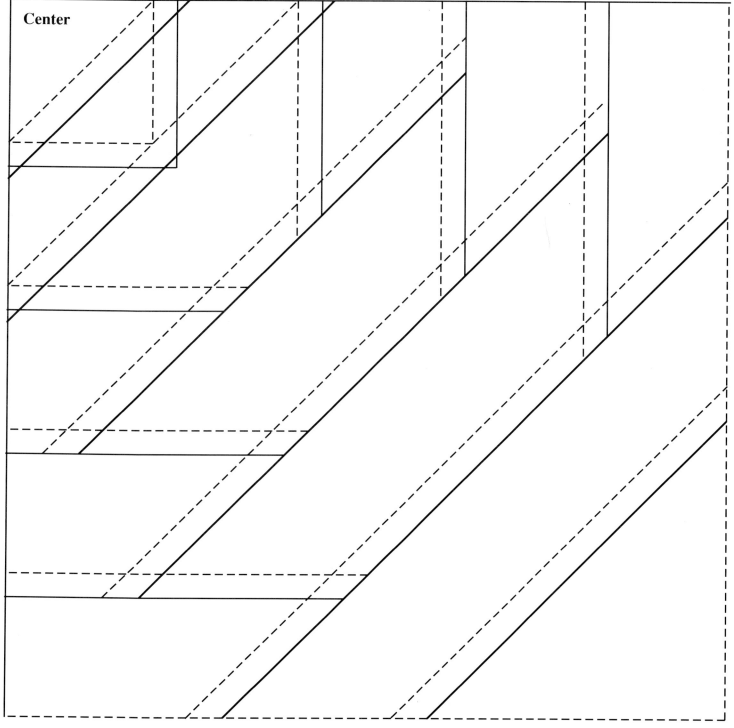

One-quarter of Pineapple Log Cabin

Center

12a

One-quarter of trapunto design for California Sunset

14a

14b

14e

14f

14g

14a 14b 14c 14d

15a

15b

Fold of fabric

15c

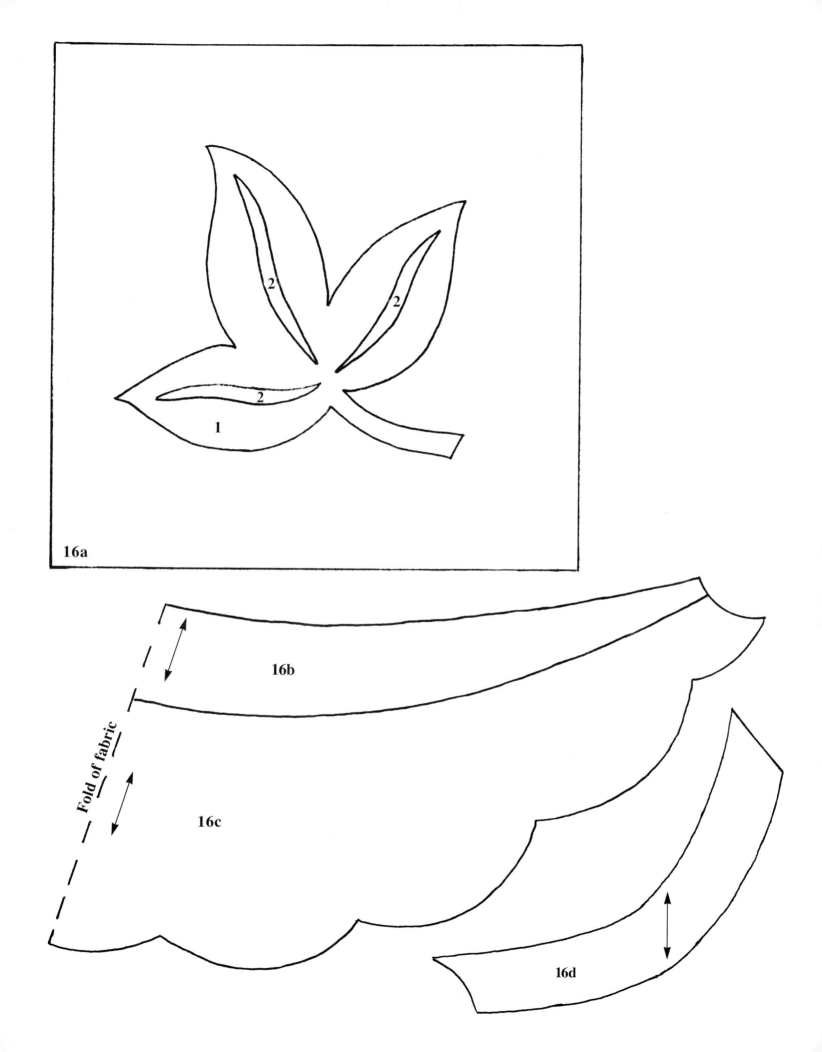

16a

2

2

2

1

16b

Fold of fabric

16c

16d

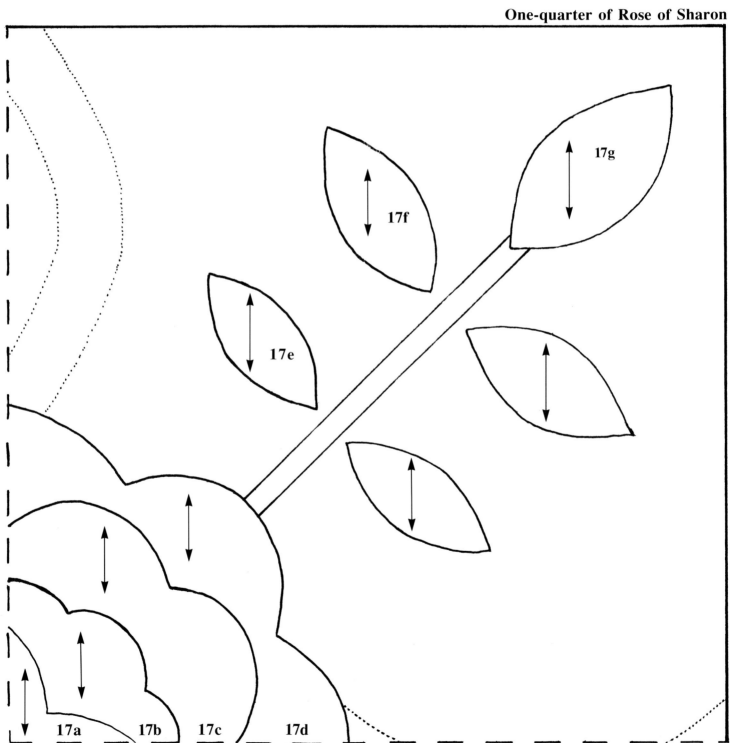

17g

17f

17e

17a   17b   17c   17d

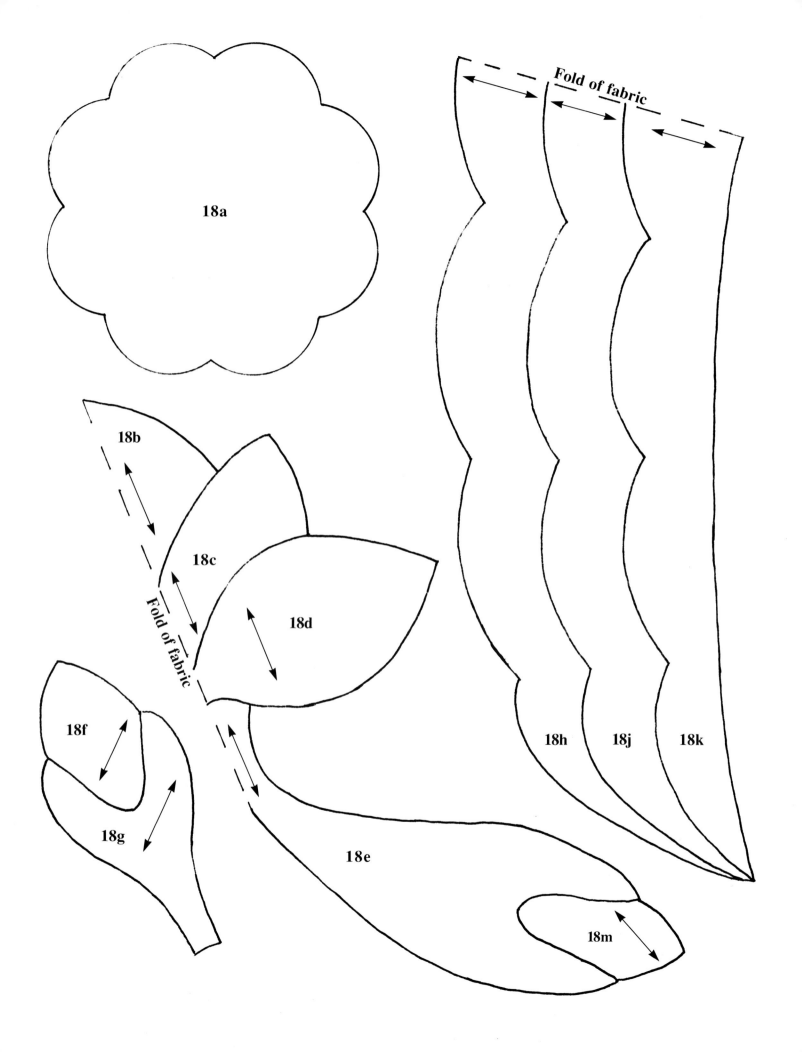

One-quarter of stenciled medallion

1

3

2

1

2

1

1

1

1

1

1

1

1

One-quarter of stenciled medallion

Registration for border. Cut edge of fabric.

20a

25a

Left swag.
Reverse stencil for
right swag.

26b

26a

Simply the Best

THE QUILT DIGEST PRESS

Dept. D
P.O. Box 1331
Gualala, CA 95445